The Point of Poetry

The Point of Poetry

Joe Nutt

Unbound

This edition first published in 2019

Unbound
6th Floor Mutual House,
70 Conduit Street,
London W1S 2GF

www.unbound.com

All rights reserved

© Joe Nutt, 2019

The right of Joe Nutt to be identified as the author of this work has been asserted in accordance with Section 77 of the Copyright, Designs and Patents Act, 1988. No part of this publication may be copied, reproduced, stored in a retrieval system, or transmitted, in any form or by any means without the prior permission of the publisher, nor be otherwise circulated in any form of binding or cover other than that in which it is published and without a similar condition being imposed on the subsequent purchaser.

Permissions and credits can be found on pages 280-1

Text design by Ellipsis, Glasgow

A CIP record for this book is available from the British Library

ISBN 978-1-78352-701-4 (hbk)
ISBN 978-1-78352-703-8 (ebook)

Printed in Great Britain by CPI Group (UK)

1 3 5 7 9 8 6 4 2

For Claire, who inadvertently gave me the idea,
and for all those who have supported the book so generously

Contents

Foreword: xi

One: 1
'Sonnet 18',
William Shakespeare

Two: 10
'The Hawk', George Mackay Brown

Three: 17
'The Tyger', William Blake

Four: 31
'The Things That Matter', E. Nesbit

Five: 42
'Adlestrop', Edward Thomas

Six: 50
'Break of Day in the Trenches', Isaac Rosenberg

Seven: 60
'When I am dead, my dearest', Christina Rossetti

Eight: 72
'Mrs Midas', Carol Ann Duffy

Nine: 85
'Tractor', Ted Hughes

Ten: 95
'My Last Duchess', Robert Browning

Eleven: 109
'To His Coy Mistress', Andrew Marvell

Twelve: 121
'Famous for What?' Hollie McNish

Thirteen: 138
'The Gun', Vicki Feaver

Fourteen: 151
'Twickenham Garden', John Donne

Fifteen: 164
'Blackberry-Picking', Seamus Heaney

Sixteen: 173
'The Darkling Thrush', Thomas Hardy

Seventeen: 184
The Rime of the Ancient Mariner, Samuel Taylor Coleridge

Eighteen: 196
The Eve of St Agnes, John Keats

Nineteen: 210
'The Bistro Styx', Rita Dove

Twenty: 221
'The Sea and the Skylark', Gerard Manley Hopkins

Twenty-One: 234
The Prelude, William Wordsworth

Twenty-Two: 258
Paradise Lost, John Milton

Where to Now?: 275

Credits: 280

Notes: 282

Acknowledgements: 286

A Note on the Author: 287

Supporters: 288

Foreword

Every Saturday morning as a child, I would climb on a bus and take a twenty-minute journey into the centre of a small Midlands town to visit the local library. Library cards, small rectangles of pastel-coloured cardboard tucked into a little wallet inside any book you wished to loan, were priceless tickets to different places, journeys only made possible because of the books stacked so neatly on those polished wooden shelves. Those cards were precious. The first responsibility I ever carried. The best part of the entire morning would be taken up reading and browsing, often kneeling on the hard parquet floor surrounded by a small heap of books, until a final choice was made and I climbed back on a bus clutching a new batch of books. To this day I have to drag myself out of any bookshop. There is something deliciously seductive about all those book spines staring at you, all the unknown worlds trapped between those hidden covers. Reading fiction is the closest you or I will ever get to time travel.

Those early books were a complete mishmash. I was as fascinated by books about practical things – sport, the countryside, flags and knots – as I was by fiction. It wasn't until early in my secondary schooling that I was properly and skilfully introduced to poetry. Like most children, I knew what verse was, of course, through nursery rhymes and songs, but this unique form of human expression, poetry, was entirely new to me, and in the hands of some skilled teachers I realised, from those initial lessons, that it mattered.

This book is for all those who never got it, those hordes of metrophobes who are perfectly happy living in cities or travelling by Tube but who, for whatever reason, poetry passed by like a bad Samaritan. Most will never even know they suffer from this common ailment, that metrophobia has nothing to do with cities or underground railways and is simply a fear of poetry. I was lucky. In my case, good teaching led to studying English literature at university, two decades teaching the subject in schools and writing books about arguably the three greatest English poets: William Shakespeare, John Donne and John Milton. But my career has been shared between schools and business, and the business half has brought me into contact with hundreds of educated, intelligent, successful adults for whom poetry remains almost anathema. Make the slightest allusion to it in conversation over a drink at a hotel bar, any evening after you've all finished sitting through meetings, editing a pack of slides or juggling figures on a spreadsheet, and you will see the fear twinkle in their eyes.

This book doesn't seek to complain about that, or to discuss the reasons why it happens. Instead what it aims to do is to show all those left sitting bruised and battered on the roadside when poetry passed them by at school what they've been missing. That's why I called the book *The Point of Poetry*.

When I taught, I inevitably found myself facing questions about what poetry was. Children like to categorise. It makes them feel safer and poetry is one of the things they struggle with. A poem is not quite a song and not quite a story. It doesn't look like anything most children are used to seeing on a page, yet it's in exactly the same language as every other lesson and textbook. Even mediocre poetry is dense and difficult. Children can't resist an urge to know what a poem *means*. At first I would answer their questions with the usual range of tactics and responses any English teacher would employ: for example, I stressed poetry was something you needed to hear aloud and listen to. But after some years, appreciating that what they needed was something to latch on to, I added something of my own. Poetry, I would say, is all about economy. Poets pack meaning into few words. No other kind of writer does this. Poems are like fireworks stuffed full, not with exotic chemicals, but with ideas. When you read them, you light the touchpaper. This book is all about lighting the touchpaper.

In it I have chosen a number of famous and not so famous poems. They stretch from Shakespeare to the present day, although instead of chronological order, I've used my teaching experience to link one poem to the next. So although looking back, a reader might be able to discern an overall movement from easy to difficult, from short to long poems, hopefully what you will feel as you read the book is a sense of growing confidence and excitement, which comes from the connections between poems and poets. Knowledge isn't built on sand, and secure steps in the right direction are better than leaps in the dark. Midway through the book you may find the journey even becomes a little bumpy where I've included two or three contemporary poems that are not easily enjoyed without facing up to some difficult hurdles for any reader. This is deliberate because it would be deceitful of me to encourage you to read and delight in poetry but only offer you poems I personally admire and value. If you accept my invitation, and I hope you do, you will inevitably read some poetry that disappoints you. In some ways it's how you react to that experience, what you stand to gain from it, that is even more valuable and significant than the pleasure to be had from reading poetry that simply delights.

There are plenty of poets who don't just toss a gauntlet down; they take a firm grip on it before whacking it across your cheek with audible relish. You can offer them the other cheek if you wish. Personally, I prefer to pick the gauntlet up, because it's then that poetry begins to impact on the language that you use and even the life that you lead. It's that intense, often provocative engagement with the way language is being used by someone else that allows you to develop and refine your own word management. We are what we eat may be how other people see us. It's what we say and what we write that determines how they feel about us.

Although many of the poems are reproduced, most of the contemporary ones are not and this is definitively not a book of literary criticism for the kind of student expecting someone else to dissect specific poems word by word for them. That's why, where they are reproduced, they appear at the end of a chapter, not the beginning. By that time, my hope is, you will be just itching to read them.

Some you may have heard of, others, almost certainly not, but for each poem I have used the same simple process of taking it as the starting point for an essay about the world we all know and live in today. That's what happens when you light the touchpaper. The poem ignites something in you about in the world you personally inhabit, the space you occupy in history and the people you have shared irreplaceable hours with. If any of these essays amuse, entertain, enlighten or delight you, then I will have done my job. But if they send you rushing to the end in search of the poem, to light its touchpaper for yourself, then I will quietly and secretly rejoice.

One

Sonnet 18
(1609)
'Shall I compare thee to a summer's day?'
William Shakespeare (1554–1616)

The first Elizabethans took poetry, like religion, seriously. English was just beginning to establish itself as a language worthy both of art and its sly sibling, diplomacy. Latin was still the language of scholarship and international relations, but with the help of less courtly, regional men like Shakespeare, English was making leaps and bounds.

Shakespeare penned a whole bundle of sonnets, poems of fourteen lines with a set pattern of rhyme conventionally used by male poets in Europe to express love, which life experience suggests is often nothing more than an adolescent crush or feverish lust. Shakespeare scholars have built entire careers around analysing these poems and, especially, arguing over who they were written for, because in the world of the Elizabethan court, poetry was frequently written and sent to real people to impress them and gain their patronage, even, on occasion, to seduce them. John Donne famously had to ask his friends for some of his poems back because he didn't keep copies. Why would he?

In recent years considerable effort has gone into arguing that Shakespeare's sonnets, all 154 of them, form an intelligible sequence and that most of them are addressed not to the *dark lady* you may well have heard of, but to a *fair youth*. Arguments about whether individual sonnets deal with heterosexual, homosexual or Platonic love are nothing new. Responding to them as a coherent sequence instead of reading the poems in isolation might be very appealing, but it relies entirely on how editors and publishers chose to number them, often many years after Shakespeare's death. I'm always suspicious that the keenest participants in these sexual debates tend to ignore the obvious reality that Shakespeare wrote some of the most astonishingly insightful plays about heterosexual love at various stages of adult life any human being has ever managed to pen. So you can see straightaway why that childhood question – what does a poem mean? – can get us into all kinds of trouble today. We have mobiles, Twitter and shifting sexual agendas and debates. They had parchment, a quill and many more hours to kill.

Read any of Shakespeare's sonnets without appreciating that one day, around 400 years ago, a real, flesh and blood Elizabethan unfolded a sheet of parchment and read it with pleasure, and you underestimate them. So when in Sonnet 18 he tells (let's assume) some young lady that she is far more *lovely* and *temperate* than a summer's day, it's a reasonable guess that she was more touched than if he'd sent her a smiley face and a dick pic.

Elizabethan court life, centred geographically on Whitehall, just as the business of government is today, was also more risky than anything the current, power-crazed occupants of Number 10 face. Catholic and Protestant political disagreements pulsed through every vein of the English state, and one wrong word or sentiment could see you face a truly unpleasant and terrible death. So what you wrote required care. You thought long and hard before committing those thoughts to parchment. Consequently, your family and friends treated mail with great respect. Think of it a bit like this. Every third contributor to any Facebook thread about Jeremy Corbyn or Theresa May would be carted away to the Tower of London for torture and an unthinkably grim public execution. We live in less violently reactive times. Now it's just Twitter and the tabloids who disembowel the innocent in public.

For generations, Sonnet 18 would have been thought of and taught as an unusually clever, heterosexual love poem, a witty rejection of the normal tactic of the lovesick poet, who worked his way with growing excitement through a list of similes about various bits of his beloved's anatomy. Hair like gold, eyes like jewels and lips like cherries. The kind of mush that reddens faces in classrooms full of adolescent hormones and undeclared passion. John Donne produced a particularly detailed, shameless version in his Elegy 19, which is guaranteed to raise a teenage blush, even in today's classrooms. Besides the fumbling, adolescent enthusiasm of *Licence my roving hands, and let them go,/Before, behind, between, above, below,* Donne's lover risks embarrassing every teenage boy battling with the temptations of pornography when he asks the girl, *As liberally, as to a Midwife, shew/Thy self: cast all, yea, this white lynen hence.*

Shakespeare shifts his ground elsewhere and builds on the initial comparison of his beloved to summer, all with the goal of winning her over at the end with a knockout compliment. The sonnet is famous for its final, brilliant assertion; that by praising her and writing about her in this poem, he has in effect, immortalised her.

So long as men can breathe, or eyes can see,
So long lives this, and this gives life to thee.

It's an impressive chat-up line, as well as a superb illustration of poetry as economics. Try turning it into workaday prose and see how long it takes you. Who wouldn't want to be remembered in this way? After all, this poem has been reprinted literally millions of times in many hundreds of poetry anthologies and collections, translated into languages as disparate as Afrikaans and Esperanto – never mind how many times it must have been downloaded in the last decade. It must have featured in countless weddings and rescued a doomed Valentine's Day as often as a bunch of flowers grabbed at the local garage, or a chicken biryani and a bottle of rosé. Shakespeare would have been out of his doublet and his love her hose before he could have dipped his quill if she'd have known he was going to make her that famous.

But here (as Will himself put it elsewhere) is the rub. We actually don't know who he wrote this sonnet for, so how on earth can we admire her? A portrait would have been handy. Even more insulting for the poor, anonymous lass, as we've seen, modern critics don't want to agree over whether it was written for a man or a woman. Now my guess is even the most liberal gentlewoman in Elizabeth's court would have come over just a bit frosty at the thought that Will's fourteen lines of literary brilliance couldn't even capture her gender.

Which points towards something critical to any understanding of what poetry is or why it matters. Like all published literature, the moment the final dot of ink stains the page, even before the finished work arrives on the library or the bookshop shelf, the poet has lost it. It's out of their control for ever. Irrespective of how much intense effort and care they invested in constructing it, how wholly in control they felt of its structure, design, content and meaning, it has a life of its own now, and they can never reclaim it. The touchpaper will be lit not once, but many, many times and all those ideas they packed into it, knowingly or unknowingly, are going to burst into someone's life somewhere, whether they like it or not, each time producing a different display.

That's a thrilling thought once you grasp all its implications. It's an amazing invitation to any reader. Like handing the tallest, most brightly coloured, fattest rocket imaginable to a child clutching a sparkler in the darkness on Bonfire Night.

It's not just the question of the lover's identity in Sonnet 18 that illustrates how true this is. Addressing that question is a pragmatic, factual, historical pathway to the poem. Right now there is probably a metrophobic project manager reading this at the same time as you on the train to work somewhere in the world thinking that, in spite of all that scholarly effort, there must be some way to identify her. But that is only one amongst limitless ways to respond to it. We can admire the skill of the rhyme. It's no mean trick to rhyme *date* with *temperate* or *shines* with *declines*. But if that doesn't tickle your fancy, there's the gentle, clever timing of the rhythm that builds to that final, dramatic couplet. That final compliment about timelessness reverberates more powerfully as a result. Or you can ponder the various clever images, those carefully chosen individual words and combinations of words that Shakespeare uses to praise her, as they appeal to you, or repel you: it is entirely your choice. The sparkler is in your hand. You can reflect on that curious choice of *untrimm'd*, a word that sounds coined and that appears to mean 'undone', but when you look into its etymological history, you discover it was specifically used around that time to describe a ship's hull that hadn't been cleaned of barnacles and seaweed. The avenues of thought open to you are endless and endlessly fascinating.

However, I'll repeat, this book was never designed to meet the needs of any formal literary student looking for forensic analysis, line by line, so although I want to alert you to the rich tapestry of detail in any poem, it's the wider, bigger picture, those startling bursts of colour at the climax of every firework display I want to dwell on and encourage you to enjoy.

Most love poetry, at least that dripping off a male pen, has a pretty basic aim in mind, however much Petrarch, Dante or even Donne try to dress it up. So much love poetry is little more than a struggle to try and describe the sensation of noticing a beautiful woman. It comes with cleverness and invention, but in the end, it's just about that moment of recognition. The poet might indulge in all kinds of mind games, deploy a whole armoury of strategies to convince the object of his affection that she is so much more than a beauty in his eyes, but so often they are fooling no one but themselves. One of the things that make Shakespeare's sonnets different, more interesting and pleasing to read, is that he seems to know that. They deal with abstract, difficult ideas to do with time, loyalty and perception. Sonnet 18 even starts with a tacit acknowledgement of this limitation in other poets by immediately rejecting the rhetorical question it opens with. *Shall I compare thee to a summer's day?* he asks, before instantly answering *no*, because she is *more lovely and more temperate*. The conventional strategy, that litany of complimentary similes, is immediately dumped in favour of something more thoughtful.

No one, except perhaps a professional trophy wife on the hunt for a frail but loaded number five, wants to be regarded as nothing more than the physical form they inhabit. And however powerful physicality is as an attracting force, it quickly takes a back seat the moment we make eye contact and someone opens their mouth to speak. We do indeed seek far more in those we fall in love with. And Shakespeare's sonnets are a delight because they *start* there.

They also lead us naturally into contemplating the whole business of developing a relationship through words. As written proof of someone's declared affection, Shakespeare's sonnets are like little experiments in persuasion, tiny windows into someone else's relationships. Read all 154 and you will struggle to find one that isn't vigorously trying to convince its recipient about something or other. In spite of the critical confidence that lumps so many sonnets together around the *fair youth*, I also defy anyone to assert they sense the same single human being is on the receiving end of all this affectionate praise and love. Poetry in Shakespeare's day was also about patronage and, as often as not, when you read any one of his sonnets, there is this nagging suspicion that it's more an exercise in flattery than a declaration of heartfelt emotion.

Apart from the pain of being coerced to write poetry in school, I suspect the only time any normal human being attempts to put something down on paper that isn't a tax form or a shopping list is when the extremity of human emotion, often love but sometimes grief, forces them to pick up a pen. However cathartic, the resulting verse is rarely edifying, but it points to an important aspect of poetry that teachers, especially, undersell. Poets have always had something of a reputation for intensity and excess. I doubt whether Sappho, Byron, Dylan Thomas or Sylvia Plath wrote many shopping lists, and I dread to think what their tax forms looked like. Of course it's foolish to generalise, unless you make someone smile, and Ms Plath might well have been every taxman's dream form-filler, but if you once perceive that poetry operates on the edges of man's knowledge and experience, that it represents in art a profoundly sincere attempt by individuals to grapple with the inexorable conditions of human life, then you are well on the way to becoming not just a reader of it but a fan.

Sonnet 18

Shall I compare thee to a summer's day?
Thou art more lovely and more temperate:
Rough winds do shake the darling buds of May,
And summer's lease hath all too short a date;
Sometime too hot the eye of heaven shines,
And often is his gold complexion dimm'd;
And every fair from fair sometime declines,
By chance or nature's changing course untrimm'd;
But thy eternal summer shall not fade,
Nor lose possession of that fair thou ow'st;
Nor shall death brag thou wander'st in his shade,
When in eternal lines to time thou grow'st:
So long as men can breathe or eyes can see,
So long lives this, and this gives life to thee.

Two

The Hawk
(1970)
George Mackay Brown (1921–96)

Poetry is undoubtedly best read aloud. Even an epic like Milton's *Paradise Lost* becomes a whole different beast when you listen to it, and there are contemporary poets who argue that to get the full, unadulterated beauty of any poem you need to hear the poet themselves read it. They probably also think Elvis is still alive. Anyone who has heard that astounding early recording of Tennyson intoning 'The Charge of the Light Brigade' like a midnight visitor at Ebenezer Scrooge's house, or heard Jeffrey Archer read any of his own literary efforts, will have their doubts as well as their scars. Even Hilary Mantel's admirable eloquence on the page can be a bit harrowing when you listen to the voice God gave her coming out of a radio. Just because you can write something doesn't mean you can read it. But one of the reasons I've chosen 'The Hawk', by the Orcadian poet George Mackay Brown, is because he is the exception that proves the rule. It is a gift to be able to read verse well and he had it, as well as an accent that is as wedded to his poetry as he was to his home. He spent almost all of his life in the small port of Stromness on Orkney's mainland, apart from brief periods studying in Scotland. Few poets' work is so deeply rooted in the soil of their birth.

I was lucky enough to spend many weeks in Orkney, staying in Stromness in a beautiful old house that had ships' masts for beams and an ancient stone construction in the garden that was an old whaling inn. Every so often an unusually high tide would seep gently and silently up through the stone walls that protected the house from the sea and flood the kitchen floor with crystal-clear, salty water. The owners kept all their kitchen equipment standing on hefty wooden boxes, just out of reach of these occasional inundations. Orkney is a windswept, treeless, remarkably exhilarating corner of Great Britain.

'The Hawk' describes seven encounters in the bird's life, on seven subsequent days, ending in its unremarkable death, shot by a crofter, Jock, concerned no doubt about his livestock. There are some spectacular birds of prey in that part of the world. The sight of large hen harriers, swooping low along fences and hovering over the heather, is not at all unusual. There are also large and aggressive great skuas, which although not hawks, are perfectly capable of killing a medium-sized mammal like a hare or rabbit and think nothing of driving you away with fierce clouts on your head with their flat feet. On one occasion on the island of Hoy, my springer spaniel picked up a huge, adult hare, still warm and limp, with a large hole in its flank I have no doubt was inflicted by a great skua. In remote fields, I've seen these huge birds shot dead, their massive wings stretched out, literally crucified on barbed wire fences. I imagine it's because some crofters think that will deter others birds from attacking lambs or chickens.

Sitting on the small ferryboat returning to Stromness, the ferryman looked at the hare for a long time and eyed my dog suspiciously, who was bursting with pride, before furrowing his weatherbeaten brow and asking, 'He's a springer spaniel?'

'Yes,' I said, 'But he's really fast.'

'The Hawk' is a poignant little poem, capturing the bird's rich life in one evocative encounter after another. A farmer's collie protects a lamb, a group of twitchers point dozens of binoculars skywards at it, and it summarily disposes of a chicken, a rabbit and a blackbird before Jock puts an end to it without a second thought. Mackay Brown has that gift of so many great poets, a near-magical grasp of metaphor, so the chicken dies *Lost in its own little snowstorm.*

It's a haggard old cliché that poets commune with nature. Wordsworth is imagined striding out, unsuitably dressed, head-first into a gale across some mountainous part of the Lake District, composing lines in his head, while Gerard Manley Hopkins goes into eco-despair over some spindly poplar trees someone cruelly chopped down without telling him. Less than ten minutes walk from where I am sitting and writing, in the corner of a large wheat field, shining in the August sun, is a tall, white alcove, open to the countryside it overlooks, a folly named locally as Cowper's Alcove, after the poet and translator of Homer, William Cowper. He frequently sat in it and enjoyed the view across the fields to the villages beyond. The natural world is as natural a source of inspiration and subject matter for poets as is love or loss. Thomas Hardy can bring a stark, rocky pathway to life and Seamus Heaney can sweep you back with him to a childhood Irish bog so vividly that you can smell the peat. One of the greatest pleasures in reading poetry is that delightful sensation you get when a writer takes you with them somewhere else, somewhere often far more beautiful, vital and, hence, memorable than your geographical reality. It's not a gift peculiar to poets, but they can do it in the blink of an eye and with far fewer words than most.

Perhaps it's therefore no surprise that raptors seem popular with poets. Anyone who spends time in the countryside can't but be impressed by the sight of any bird of prey hunting. Tennyson's snapshot 'The Eagle' is as striking and succinct as the brushwork of an oriental calligrapher. Gerard Manley Hopkins's 'The Windhover' is simply stunning in its capturing of the complex, distinctive manoeuvres of a kestrel in flight, quite an achievement in a poem about Jesus Christ. Ted Hughes, in contrast, goes for the less exciting image of a 'Hawk Roosting', yet ends up turning it into the most frightening symbol of nature's utter thoughtlessness and amoral beauty. George Mackay Brown's treatment, is workaday, matter-of-fact, a relaxed acceptance of life as he knew it was lived in Orkney. His hawk is just one character in an everyday Orcadian story.

One of the most consequential aspects of contemporary living is that quite recently mankind turned a historic corner and for the first time in human evolution, most of us now live in cities. If you are one of those fortunate individuals for whom the four seasons isn't a hotel chain or a vintage rock band, then you will probably find 'The Hawk' and the entire genre of natural poetry it belongs to easier to read and more appealing. If the closest you come to the natural world is gazing out of a train window at uncontrolled and unidentifiable vegetable matter interspersed with leftovers from Network Rail as you commute to the office every morning, then you may well struggle. But then that's one reason why I wrote this book. Wordsworth striding up that hill and Gerard Manley Hopkins blubbing at his pet poplar stumps were doing something we all probably need but most of us fail to do. They were thinking deeply about the physical and intellectual world in which every second of all our lives is spent. And wallowing up to their necks in it, swimming around in all that fresh air, low cloud and frolicking fauna, is one of the most powerful ways to link the two, the physical and the intellectual.

I, for one, am grateful to those who do haul their backsides out there in all weathers, amidst all that vigour and vitality, and write about the world we share with those other life forms in verse. I know it's not something I can do and I also know that there are poets whose reflections on what they see and experience crashing through the heather, or sitting beneath lofty foliage, can enrich my own world view. One of the most persuasive art theorists I have ever read, the Russian Formalist Viktor Shklovskii, argued that art existed 'so that stones may be made stony'. The poet's skill is in making us look at the world anew, through different, less tainted lenses. Everyday life corrodes things, Shklovskii argued. It neuters and greys-out things, renders them dull and uninspiring, whether they are the simplest of material objects, or the most subtle of emotions. All succumb to the same erosion. Poets are nature's art restorers.

'The Hawk' doesn't apotheosise the bird. George Mackay Brown isn't Albrecht Dürer painting a young hare so lifelike you sense its timidity. For him the bird is an everyday sight, something to be seen seven days a week, like the sea or the heather outside his home. What strikes me about the poem is the calm acceptance of death. He weaves it into the rhythm and fabric of the verse without fuss or drama. It's the natural conclusion to a life led killing other things, neither sad nor tragic, just real. But like all great firework displays, something special is saved for the end and he gives us the space and quiet that follows to think about the poem's only human character, Jock, and the reason or lack of reason that makes him lift that gun so nonchalantly. Without that pensive ending, 'The Hawk' could so easily become every urban environmentalist's anthem, a plaintive hymn about man's inhumanity to fluffy stuff.

The Hawk

On Sunday the hawk fell on Bigging
And a chicken screamed
Lost in its own little snowstorm.
And on Monday he fell on the moor
And the Field Club
Raised a hundred silent prisms.
And on Tuesday he fell on the hill
And the happy lamb
Never knew why the loud collie straddled him.
And on Wednesday he fell on a bush
And the blackbird
Laid by his little flute for the last time.
And on Thursday he fell onCleat
And peerie Tom's rabbit
Swung in a single arc from shore to hill.
And on Friday he fell on a ditch
But the rampant rat,
The eye and the tooth, quenched his flame.
And on Saturday he fell on Bigging
And Jock lowered his gun
And nailed a small wing over the corn.

Three

The Tyger
(1794)
William Blake (1757–1827)

Most children who have attended school in an English-speaking country with a functioning state education system will have seen this poem. So I imagine it has a lot to do with why so many successful adults end up hating poetry. William Blake probably features on every metrophobe's hit list, even those who will belt out 'Jerusalem' at a rugby match or on far less religious occasions, perhaps in adult life unaware that Blake was responsible for both these building blocks of English classrooms worldwide.

The poem is only six short verses long but contains no less than eleven separate questions beginning with 'What?', all of them attempting to understand the mind of God. I said earlier, in my introduction to these essays, I had learned at school that poetry matters. 'The Tyger' is my first attempt to really convince you of that.

To a child just about coping with the difference between *advice* and *advise* or even *have* and *of*, spelling Tyger with a 'y' is just confirmation that any poet's main mission is to sow confusion and doubt. The barrage of rhetorical questions that makes up most of the poem piles on the agony and it's easy to see why so many children might respond perfectly well to a brightly coloured illustration of the poem without even beginning to grasp a single idea it contains. Even if they know something about the book of Genesis and quickly get the idea in the poem's first verse of God creating the tiger and designing its *fearful symmetry*, to any child trying gamely to grasp the concept of symmetry in their maths class, illustrations that show a tiger sideways on are just plain cruel. Think of all those diagonals. If you were one of those children, forget everything you felt about the poem in the past.

Blake was, of course, an artist as well as a poet, although, strictly speaking, he was an engraver, and when you look at his own illustration for 'The Tyger' from his book, *Songs of Experience*, also sideways on, it doesn't exactly fill you with confidence he knew anything about big cats. Blake's tiger is a vastly oversized, overweight moggy, grinning comically, as if on its way to meet Alice and the Dormouse for tea and some more of those yummy toasted muffins. This always makes me wonder if Blake had ever seen a tiger himself, face first, as it were.

Critics and later fans love to describe Blake as a visionary, which has the advantage of being literally true, since he saw visions throughout his life, and they played a key part in his art. Just take a look at his illustration *The Day of Judgement* for Robert Blair's poem *The Grave*, or anything at all he produced to illustrate Milton's *Paradise Lost*. So it is perhaps naïve to even suggest he would be interested in depicting a tiger naturally. Wordsworth was convinced Blake was mad, and the astonishing variety of revolutionary and radical thinkers and thoughts Blake toyed with throughout his life certainly don't point to a man of great intellectual stability. He wore the red floppy hat popular with French revolutionaries ... and Noddy, until news of Madame Guillotine's excessive appetite turned his stomach. He spent his life entirely in London, with a spell in Sussex, so it's fruitless to look for natural beauty or insight in a poem like 'The Tyger', as we might in anything by George Mackay Brown. Although the obvious word *jungle* was certainly available to Blake as an import from early British adventures in India, he opts for the temperate *forests* instead, as though he wanted his tiger to be stalking the English countryside alongside Robin Hood.

The more one thinks about it, the more one wonders why on earth any sane English teacher would let 'The Tyger' loose on a classroom full of children. A. A. Milne's Tigger is a far safer playmate. For all his interest in childhood and innocence, Blake's imagination is ruthlessly adult. He devoted his life to new ideas and social change, surrounding himself with experimental materials and minds. There is so little for a real child, even a teenager, to access in any of his verse.

Historically, the way the poem found its way into anthologies and then classrooms was almost certainly through well-intentioned Christianity; decent, church-going Anglicans looking to educate village idiots before Darwin came along and upset the vital part church or chapel played in village life. If you want children to take the book of Genesis literally – and

Blake was an ardent, if unconventional Christian, writing fifty years before *The Origin of Species* appeared – then framing that question, 'Did the guy in the sky who made the tiger really also make the lamb?' rhetorically is well nigh essential.

To enjoy reading 'The Tyger' today, however badly you were mauled by it as a child, you are more likely to enjoy Blake's impressive and possibly intuitive view of the animal's strength and beauty than anything else. Searching for the opposite of the Christian symbol of humility and self-sacrifice, the lamb, Blake spurns the wolf or lion, and even the most obvious candidate, a serpent, settling instead on a creature that in today's world quite credibly screams intelligent design. In that case, 'visionary' starts to become less of a joke. Blake's tiger burns brightly in the night. Even its eyes burn and everything about it is fierce and deadly. He successfully makes it the absolute antithesis of a lamb.

Yet when you read the poem closely, or hear those repeated sounds of fire and force as they beat relentlessly along with the poem's simple rhythm and tight rhyme – the anvils and the furnaces, the hammers and the chains, all that beating of metal on metal – you can't fail to connect it with the dramatically changing world Blake knew, the Industrial Revolution he often wrote about and decried, because it seemed to him to steal so much away from people. Blake's tiger is in the end not a natural phenomenon, but an industrial creation like his illustration of it, designed and created out of raw material, only with superhuman skill.

'The Tyger' doesn't imagine a simple scale of mammals, with

the tiger at one end and the lamb at the other; it hammers home the theodicean question that frustrates monotheistic believers everywhere: what kind of a deity creates evil?

It would be seriously underestimating the man to think none of this mattered to Blake. One of his close followers, the artist George Richmond, described Blake's death in 1827 in a letter: 'Just before he died . . . he burst out singing of the things he saw in Heaven'. Blake has the doubtful distinction of being thought a saint by the notorious occultist, Aleister Crowley, which is not an honour I suspect he would have been eager to embrace since, as we've already noted, in life he was a passionate, if unorthodox, Christian. Even from Blake's point of view, Crowley would have seemed a bit of a clown, although that seems pleasantly appropriate when you know more about the circus that formed Blake's artistic circle. Blake genuinely believed archangels inspired his work and told friends that he communicated with dead people on a fairly regular basis. So those big questions he asks in 'The Tyger' are not the least academic, or childish, to him.

If Blake's deep thinking about 'The Tyger' excites or interests you, then you will almost certainly want to get your claws into another big cat poem, Ted Hughes's 'The Jaguar'. It's fascinating to compare these two famous poems. Hughes's Jaguar also suffers from incendiary sight. Hughes even calls his feline a *visionary*, and when you reach the poem's final verse you realise that, sadly, this particular animal is probably insane, imagining itself striding through wild open spaces instead of stumbling repeatedly across the cramped confines of its cage. Anyone who has seen a beautiful, wild animal of any kind pacing incessantly behind dark bars can't fail but feel moved.

The comparison points towards something seriously significant if what you want to do is overcome a deep-rooted suspicion or fear of poetry. Poets – indeed all writers, no matter how bizarre the rituals they might follow to get themselves into the mood – don't work in a vacuum. What they have read and enjoyed, what has impressed or stayed with them, consciously or unconsciously, from other books, other poems, pulses through their own work and gives it life, whether they like it or not. The skill of other poets floods the veins of Shakespeare and Dr Seuss alike. A poem, however unique and strange, however pure and white the page it sits on, doesn't enter your life unaccompanied. It comes surrounded by literary echoes and memories, loaded with the past. That's why you get better at understanding them, why you enjoy them more, the more you read.

If you listen to someone skilfully reading 'The Tyger', I'd be surprised if you don't find yourself thinking, along with the poet, what kind of imagination could have created this ridiculously beautiful but terrifying creature? Blake's 'what' questions come so quick and fast it's impossible to reflect on or try to answer them. Instead we are pushed into thinking like the poet, into confronting that monotheistic dilemma head on. What's remarkable about this is that, unlike William, whose world was weighed down with biblical stories and whose day-to-day life was a dialogue with God, we know all about evolution. We know that this massive orange and black, stripy predator with the enviable fur coat is an unusual survivor from an ancient world, just one of a whole range of large, cat-like mammals that have come and gone through millennia while vast oceans, forests and ice sheets have ebbed and flowed around them. We *know* the tiger wasn't forged in the mind of God and hammered out on his anvil. Blake didn't.

For him there was both an act of creation and an act of choice. Doesn't that pick the poem up, shake it in every direction and dump it back down in your lap in a completely different shape? Blake really was asking that profoundly difficult theodicean question of his maker and the tiger's maker. 'The Tyger' teaches a crucial lesson for anyone wanting to enjoy poetry – indeed any literature; a lesson that is plainly and disturbingly lost on far too many students padding around university campuses today, certainly in the UK and USA, who object angrily to ideas expressed in the past that offend their modern sensibilities. You can't weigh up the ideas of the past with contemporary scales. You have to step inside the past first, use the tools they used and work with what they knew, not with what they didn't. If you express anger towards eighteenth-century Bristol merchants or Southern slave owners *per se*, what can you possibly have to say of value about sixth-century Athens, Rome or any other culture dependent on slave economies? That's why the exceptions, the William Wilberforces, Oskar Schindlers and Spartacuses of this world, surface and merit our respect.

You can see Blake was a profoundly Christian thinker just from this poem alone. If you never read another poem he ever wrote, the minute and calligraphic 'The Sick Rose', any of the

Songs of Innocence and Experience or *The Book of Urizen*, you can see from 'The Tyger' that this man worshipped an Old Testament God who wouldn't look out of place in a Bible Belt bookshop or in Charlton Heston's dressing room. If he appeared over the reader's shoulder clutching a lightning bolt or a dozen commandments no one would be surprised. His list of questions reverberates with awe and admiration. This is a God of *dread* and *dare*.

> *What the anvil? what dread grasp,*
> *Dare its deadly terrors clasp!*

Behind all those 'whats' is a shrinking, fragile, Christian soul that knows its place.

Some overtly Christian poets, like Gerard Manley Hopkins, Christina Rossetti and George Herbert, may know their place, but their love of God is as powerful and visible as their fear. Blake quakes and quivers by comparison. The climactic moment in 'The Tyger' comes when he imagines the end of the war in heaven, that moment when Satan is banished and God assumes his throne once more, supremely powerful, and eternally unassailable.

> *When the stars threw down their spears*
> *And water'd heaven with their tears:*
> *Did he smile his work to see?*
> *Did he who made the Lamb make thee?*

Man, made in God's image, is there in that shocking *smile*, a brilliantly human detail that rocks you on your heels, coming as it does immediately after the immensity of angels' tears watering heaven. The poet can barely believe it. That little *smile* demands you think about it too, and all it implies.

The answer is of course, yes. Blake knew his God created both lamb and tiger: man and mountain. However timid he sounds, he doesn't shrink in the end from the conclusion his Christian faith demands of him. It is through awe that Blake finds meaning. The tiger is an astonishingly marvellous creation, something to be marvelled at, however cruel or inimical it may act towards man. It is evidence of genius, of design, of a creator. No surprise then that today, when a theory of intelligent design has itself evolved from the slime of US creationism, Blake is generally regarded by critics and academics as a man way ahead of his time.

In the two decades I spent teaching English, one of the things I devoted a good deal of thought and effort to was choosing books that children in their first years of secondary schooling might enjoy. It depends, of course, in which kind of school you work, but schools are generally inept at making these kinds of choices. Teachers have no training in budgeting or cost control, so as educational publishers know to their dismay, they tend to spend money the day before they are told they have to, and on whatever they bought last year. I once worked in a school where the English department had a storeroom packed with pristine, unused copies of novels. All stacked neatly and alphabetically on shelves too high to reach without a chair. When I asked if I could give some of them out, I was told no. The kids would only lose them.

I was lucky enough to spend most of my career in the other kind of school, a school where books were there to be read, and where senior colleagues allowed and encouraged me to experiment with the books I chose. I never quite warmed to the contemporary novels schools and other teachers commonly used for these age groups. They always seemed a bit too preachy to me.

I played around a lot with different writers and books and, in all that time, I only found one book that I could almost guarantee would grip any boy or girl aged between about eleven and thirteen, whatever their background, reading skill or taste. Curiously enough, it's a book about tigers.

Jim Corbett was a colonel in the British army stationed in India in the 1920s and '30s who gave his name to a national park there that today has over 200 square miles dedicated to preserving the Bengal tiger. Quite something for a man who shot a lot of them. Corbett was a typical product of the British Empire: born and educated in India, the child of an ex-military officer turned minor civil servant, he grew up destined for the army, and although he had all the benefits of a good education, he spent a Mowgli kind of upbringing in the wild and became an expert naturalist almost by accident. In northern India in the 1920s, he was also very unusual in that he owned several guns, the prime reason local residents turned to him for help whenever a tiger or a leopard developed a taste for indolent human beings instead of antelope or other bouncy critters.

His book, *Man-Eaters of Kumaon,* a bestseller in its time, but out of print when I first came across a copy in a second-hand bookshop, is one of the most astonishing things I will ever read. In it Corbett describes hunting and killing a number of man-eating tigers and leopards, usually with the help of his springer spaniel, Robin, and usually at great personal and canine risk. One thing he learned about man-eaters is that once, for whatever reason, usually age or injury, they get a taste for people instead of other meat, they develop a habit to rival the most ardent crackhead. The first infamous man-eater Corbett killed had dined out on 436 men, women and children before he turned it into a rug. In Indian mountain villages in the 1920s, once a tiger decided it wasn't afraid of human beings, and that they were tastier and less frolicsome than the usual, more hirsute mains on the jungle menu, there wasn't much to stop it except the guns of Colonel Corbett. And he was frequently several hundred miles away. These mercifully rare man-eaters would stroll into villages in broad daylight and help themselves to the slowest snack, however many sticks and stones a few brave souls threw at them.

Corbett is one of the most disingenuous authors I've ever come across and writes almost as though he was producing a lengthy essay for his English teacher at the hill-station school he attended in Nainital. The book is an absolute delight, and even the most streetwise, city-bred child, who thinks Peruvian bears really do eat marmalade sandwiches and who wouldn't know the difference between a Womble and a wombat, succumbs to its charm, adventure and simplicity. In the end, Corbett spent so much time studying and understanding these unusual creatures that he became their greatest fan and protector, taking to the camera to capture their beauty and behaviour for others to appreciate and value.

He also just happened to be staying at the famous Tree Tops Hotel in Kenya when Princess Elizabeth, now Queen Elizabeth II, discovered her father had died, which prompted Corbett to write this in the hotel's visitors' book:

> *For the first time in the history of the world, a young girl climbed into a tree one day a Princess, and after having what she described as her most thrilling experience, she climbed down from the tree the next day a Queen—God bless her.*

You see what I mean about disingenuous.

Unlike Corbett, Blake is never an easy read. His poetry, however childlike and slight it may appear on the page, is often dense and difficult, sometimes consciously obscure and often just plain weird. But he hasn't gained the reputation he now has, number 38 in the BBC's list of 100 Greatest Britons, if the oscillating Wikipedia is to be believed, without there being something there worth investigating. Like so many poets, he was a man who fought constantly to understand the world — and especially the age he lived in — better, and rattled and riven by the industrial revolution as it was, his era posed anyone with half a brain some timeless gems.

The Tyger

Tyger Tyger, burning bright,
In the forests of the night;
What immortal hand or eye,
Could frame thy fearful symmetry?

In what distant deeps or skies.
Burnt the fire of thine eyes?
On what wings dare he aspire?
What the hand, dare seize the fire?

And what shoulder, & what art,
Could twist the sinews of thy heart?
And when thy heart began to beat,
What dread hand? & what dread feet?

What the hammer? what the chain,
In what furnace was thy brain?
What the anvil? what dread grasp,
Dare its deadly terrors clasp!

When the stars threw down their spears
And water'd heaven with their tears:
Did he smile his work to see?
Did he who made the Lamb make thee?

Tyger Tyger burning bright,
In the forests of the night:
What immortal hand or eye,
Dare frame thy fearful symmetry?

Four

The Things That Matter
(1905)
E. Nesbit (1858–1924)

Edith Nesbit was an Edwardian author famous for writing children's books. *Five Children and It, The Phoenix and the Carpet* and, above all, *The Railway Children* are just a few of her gifts to happy families the world over, and some would say she invented the children's novel. Certainly there are plenty of well-known children's authors today who clearly grew up, and probably threw up, entirely unintentionally as children do, on her work. She is better known as a novelist and even as a socialist, than a poet, but this particular poem of hers is a favourite with many people, and rightly so. Today, the English working class is more used to having its voice ignored, especially by socialists, than accurately reflected, but in this poem Nesbit gets as close to the real thing as Dickens and Hardy do in their fiction.

Nesbit actually established the Fabian Society, that veritable rock of the distinctly rocky modern Labour Party, on rather naïve personal foundations, together with her husband, Hubert Bland, who, like so many politically radical artists with a taste for public policy, imposed somewhat narrower policies on his family life. The details provide imaginative territory for left-leaning biographers, but just to give you a feel, besides getting his mother's paid companion pregnant while courting Edith, after Edith lost their second child a few years later, he impregnated her friend, Alice Hoatson, who had come to look after her, and from then on the Bland household became one big, happy, ménage à trois. Edith brought Alice's child Rosamund up as her own daughter, although the true nature of Hubert's promiscuity wasn't lost on their children, because as an adult Rosamund said, 'He endowed every affair with the romance of his own imagination . . . Chiefly through fantasy, perhaps, but what more powerful factor is there in a woman's life, and certainly at that period, than that of fantasy?'

Champagne socialism clearly has deep roots and wasn't invented in sixties Hampstead. Courtesy of the profits from Edith's writing, the Blands held parties and pageants at their grand house, Well Hall in south London, for members of the Fabian Society. Writers George Bernard Shaw and H. G. Wells were regulars, and Wells even tried to run off with Rosamund, but their elopement was curtailed by a punch thrown by her father at Paddington Station. I guess seduction was a less amusing pastime when the object was his own child. It is so tempting to dwell further on Nesbit's lifestyle and politics, but it's 'The Things that Matter' I'm interested in.

You will be able to find audio versions of it online easily, and the best, like the Poetry Archive's, understand how important it is to have a credible working-class voice deliver it. Nesbit deliberately adopts a form of informal, rural English that identifies the speaker instantly as an elderly countrywoman. She uses *as* where more formal English would require *that*, misses the endings off some words, says *gell* for *girl*, *'em* instead of *them* and adds *a* to *smiling* in the style of country dwellers *a-smiling* everywhere.

I'm not a linguist, so I don't know how historically accurate or faux-folksy Nesbit's rendering of her character's language is, but I like to give her the benefit of the doubt and it is similar to the kind of rural dialect you hear in Hardy's poetry or other writers renowned for their accuracy. It certainly enriches the poem and is a key reason I find myself moved by the old woman's plain speaking. Wordsworth famously argued that poetry should use the 'real language of men', one of many things he and fellow poet Samuel Taylor Coleridge must have batted back and forth across the dining table at Dove Cottage over a tankard or two of foaming ale on many a long winter's eve, while frost fell on mountain and moor, and Wordsworth's sister Dorothy settled into a settle to sew. (Folksy is dreadfully contagious, as we'll come to discover later in this chapter.)

Nesbit's poem is a simple monologue in which an old woman reflects on the valuable knowledge her long life has taught her, and is saddened at the thought it might all be lost with her death.

> *Now that I've nearly done my days,*
> *And grown too stiff to sweep or sew,*
> *I sit and think, till I'm amaze,*
> *About what lots of things I know:*

There follows a long list of things she knows, most domestic and practical, to do with food and family. Some she feels have been written down and captured by others, but some have not. These are the more mysterious results of her lived experience. Things only the kind of life she has led could have taught. She calls these *more important things* and they include things like how to choose and cook good food, *apples*, *bacon* and *peas* but also more powerful, poignant ideas like *how to get a child asleep* and *if sick men are going to die.*

With the kind of socialist fondness guaranteed to fondue the all-too-plastic hearts of luvvies everywhere, the poem sets out to praise and admire the old woman, as though what she has learned is as valuable and important as the stuff of more formal education. There is a championing of the working class going on which at the time would have still been quite unusual. Nesbit wrote this almost a decade before D. H. Lawrence's sons in *Sons and Lovers* started climbing a social ladder only put in front of them because their fictional mother forced a formal education upon them.

Yet when you listen to the poem, it's difficult to resist the speaker's sincerity. Nesbit successfully captures something genuine here and we don't doubt this woman knows what she says she knows, even when her knowledge counters simple science. Speaking of young wives, for example, she claims to know *what sort of times they'll have,/And if they'll have a boy or gell.* The piling on of one piece of knowledge after another, the list form Nesbit adopts for the poem, helps to generate that sense of trust, and together with the gentle, humble tone she gives the woman, we come to believe in her completely. Which is why as the poem reaches its climax, it becomes something quite different and impressive.

As she builds up in her own mind the wealth of knowledge she has accrued, aware as she is of her age and frailty, that it should all vanish with her *when I'm fast down in the clay*, the idea becomes both distressing and wasteful, *Forgetting seems such silly waste!* That all this accumulated knowledge, all these practical and subtle pearls of wisdom life has strung around her neck, will be scattered and lost for ever, that *the Angels will make haste/To dust it all away with wings!* leads as much to a question of faith as Blake's relentless list of 'whats' in 'The Tyger'. In the final few lines, 'The Things that Matter' takes on the nature of a type of prayer common in poetry and religious ritual, the intercession.

> *O God, you made me like to know,*
> *You kept the things straight in my head,*
> *Please God, if you can make it so,*
> *Let me know something when I'm dead.*

What began as a slight and perhaps curious dramatic monologue turns into the profound desire of one soul to appease an omnipotent, omniscient, implacably Christian God in the face of death. In that wistful, wishful last line lies a quintessentially human yearning for continuity beyond the grave. And behind the first two lines, which acknowledge and accept that all her wisdom has been a gift from God – *O God, you made me like to know/You kept the things straight in my head* – is the same desperate desire to understand we saw in Blake. The poem's inconsequential little title ends up shouldering something of far grander significance. Poets, at least the best of them, do deal in things that matter.

I suspect Edith Nesbit would find the gulf that exists between the rural working class she championed in a poem like 'The Things that Matter' and their social equivalent in Britain today baffling. She would have been less confused by mainstream media and other voices keen to point out the working class's lack of education after a referendum result the educated classes found hard to swallow. Yet Nesbit, I think, would be more understanding of its contemporary causes.

One of the least well understood or openly discussed aspects of the way many artists and writers worldwide regard a working class they've decided to champion but who are entirely foreign to them, is just how pungently patronising they are. It runs through their art and literature like the veins of mould in a particularly whiffy cheese. It's visible in the angular muscularity of socialist realism depicting Soviet workers waving flags, in the physical passion (and lust) so many of D. H. Lawrence's characters exhibit, and even creeps into the decent simple-mindedness of Edith Nesbit's old woman. I blame William Morris.

One of the least successful, at least in terms of literature, but arguably most influential of all socialist artists, Morris made a name for himself as a key figure in the Arts and Crafts Movement that blossomed around 1900, and his influence on design is all around us even today. He was offered the job as Poet Laureate but turned it down because it clashed with his political stance as a republican. He exemplifies this particular cultural phenomenon. From a wealthy, upper-middle-class family, he studied Classics at Oxford and founded a successful business, but fell in love with a real working-class girl, a story that speaks eloquently to a modern political obsession, social mobility. A close look at Dante Gabriel Rossetti's famous painting of the other Dante's *Beatrice* or his *Proserpine* will add flesh to these scant bones, since Morris's wife, Jane Burden, was in every sense the artist's model. Her fraught relationships with Morris and Rossetti lurked beneath the surface of the Pre-Raphaelite movement before the paint was wet.

For all Morris's sympathy with ordinary 'folk', his business relied on them and employed them as workers, yet in his entire body of poetry, prose and artwork, Morris is as alien to them as Trump is to trailer trash. For readers of Tolkien or even *Game of Thrones* fans, it's hard to stomach Morris's writing today. All that well-wrought ironwork and strapping leather, those buxom wenches and stout yeoman; it's enough to make you swap your flagon of mead for a dry martini. A naïve romanticism is always what really what lurks behind these middle-class efforts to get back to nature. It's not far beneath the surface even in the works of that talented novelist, D. H. Lawrence, who was at least the genuine article: a working-class lad from the pits.

One final postscript on this disruptive class disconnect, which still plays out in British cultural and political life today. For all her admiration of the old woman, the depth and richness of her humanity, her priceless domestic knowledge and experience, Nesbit exhibited little of it herself. Her son Fabian suffered from ill health and when he was aged fifteen, his parents agreed with the doctor he should have his tonsils removed. The operation was carried out at the family home, Well Hall. Fabian was anaesthetised and the doctor, confident the operation had been successful, left him in the care of his loving parents. Fabian died. His mother had tried to warm his sleeping body with candles and hot-water bottles, totally unaware that he had choked on his own vomit because she had forgotten to do as she had been told by the doctor and make sure he didn't eat for twenty-four hours before the operation.

The Things That Matter

Now that I've nearly done my days,
And grown too stiff to sweep or sew,
I sit and think, till I'm amaze,
About what lots of things I know:
Things as I've found out one by one –
And when I'm fast down in the clay,
My knowing things and how they're done
Will all be lost and thrown away.

There's things, I know, as won't be lost,
Things as folks write and talk about:
The way to keep your roots from frost,
And how to get your ink spots out.
What medicine's good for sores and sprains,
What way to salt your butter down,
What charms will cure your different pains,
And what will bright your faded gown.

But more important things than these,
They can't be written in a book:
How fast to boil your greens and peas,
And how good bacon ought to look;
The feel of real good wearing stuff,
The kind of apple as will keep,
The look of bread that's rose enough,
And how to get a child asleep.

Whether the jam is fit to pot,
Whether the milk is going to turn,
Whether a hen will lay or not,
Is things as some folks never learn.
I know the weather by the sky,
I know what herbs grow in what lane;
And if sick men are going to die,
Or if they'll get about again.

Young wives come in, a-smiling, grave,
With secrets that they itch to tell:
I know what sort of times they'll have,
And if they'll have a boy or gell.
And if a lad is ill to bind,
Or some young maid is hard to lead,
I know when you should speak 'em kind,
And when it's scolding as they need.

I used to know where birds ud set,
And likely spots for trout or hare,
And God may want me to forget
The way to set a line or snare;
But not the way to truss a chick,
To fry a fish, or baste a roast,
Nor how to tell, when folks are sick,
What kind of herb will ease them most!

The Things That Matter

Forgetting seems such silly waste!
I know so many little things,
And now the Angels will make haste
To dust it all away with wings!
O God, you made me like to know,
You kept the things straight in my head,
Please God, if you can make it so,
Let me know something when I'm dead.

Five

Adlestrop
(1917)
Edward Thomas (1878–1917)

This short poem is one of very few that has somehow earned itself a status even greater than its author's own name. It's so powerfully capable of standing on its own feet, it will make an appearance on BBC radio or in *Country Life* magazine whenever someone's looking longingly at what it used to feel like to be English. It's simply so famous; ironically, you will almost certainly find it comes manacled to that excruciatingly inappropriate epithet beloved of idle journalists and sports commentators alike, 'iconic'. When footballers become 'iconic', the devotional religious paintings of the Greek Orthodox Church sound like little more than doodles. To call 'Adlestrop' iconic is like describing Jesus as a faith healer.

The poem describes the moment when a train stopped briefly at a tiny village station called Adlestrop, in the Cotswolds, in 1914. Even in that lean sentence you have four essentially English hallmarks – train, village, Cotswolds and 1914 – lined up in a neat row, as on the base of some anodyne silver sporting trophy, shelved but unloved inside a public-school cabinet.

The name itself, Adlestrop, reverberates Englishness. In the blink of an eye it conjures up Norman church and rustic inn, village green and thatched cottages, like an inflatable film set designed especially for *Midsomer Murders*. I've made the point several times about how important it is, if you want to enjoy them, to listen to poems. Driving through a series of country lanes in Sussex a few years ago in the early summer, on my way to a village school right on the south coast, I had the pleasure of listening to an episode of *Desert Island Discs*, which featured the record producer, Robin Millar. I've never been a pop music fan. I somehow skipped over that entire rite of passage as a teenager, yet Millar's choices of music and his justification for each track was simply enthralling. Here was a man who knew what he was talking about, literally. One of his choices was the opening to 'Gimme Shelter' by the Rolling Stones, before which Millar said this: 'If you don't want to play air rhythm guitar and be Keith Richard when you're playing this, there's no hope for you.' If you listen to 'Adlestrop' being read aloud and don't instantly grasp why it helps to hear a poem, equally, there's no hope for you.

Thomas's lovely, lyrical poem simply doesn't work unless you get the essential idea that the way a poem sounds is a vital part of its art. Even the action this poem describes, its little narrative, depends totally on sound. Steam engines, to those not old enough to have experienced them before the Beeching cuts, which wiped Adlestrop and hundreds of other placid rural stations off the map, were noisy, smoky, steam-billowing brutes that shook the platform you stood on as they pulled into it. When they left, steam thumped out of their guts in a slow *accelerando* that matched the turning of their huge, steel wheels, in such a distinctively rhythmical way, it has become a kind of sound recordist's metonym for the entire age of steam. In the still moment between the train's arrival and departure at tiny Adlestrop, Thomas has the chance to look at, and listen to, the summer scene outside his carriage window. But 'Adlestrop' captures much more.

No one gets on or gets off the train. The platform is *bare* and Thomas sees little more than the station's name, Adlestrop, which he repeats because he has a poet's ear and is acutely aware of just how potent that curious combination of syllables sounds. Read the word aloud to yourself for a moment. Adlestrop. Go on, be confident, I bet only the dog is listening, and probably snoring. Listen to the richness, the complexity of that sound.

The only other things to catch his eye were the *willows, willow-herb, and grass,/And meadowsweet, and haycocks dry*, common as muck in the English countryside even today, if you except the *haycocks*. Meadowsweet is a tall herb with small, creamy white flowers that appreciates the damp, while willow-herb flowers, also lovers of waste ground, are a livid, pale mauve colour, like the most common shade of rhododendrons you see in English country-house gardens. It has an interesting association with railways, because it was quite a rare plant until the expansion of railways encouraged its spread. During the war it was called bombweed because it grew quickly on bomb craters, and any British commuter dependent on Network Rail should be familiar with it today since, together with abandoned sleepers, long lengths of rusty rail and assorted sacks of ballast, it is perhaps the most common sight out of a carriage window, besides graffiti.

These plants are *No whit less still and lonely fair/Than the high cloudlets in the sky*. I suspect one of the more subtle reasons behind the poem's appeal lies in the way the English long for the summer, for those rare *cloudlets*. I'm writing in mid-May and the rain is coming down outside the window in front of me absolutely vertically, like broken pencil lines drawn with a ruler. Dozens of tiny water bombs explode per second on the metallic surface of the garden table, while the sky above the hedge I can see is one single, solid mass of stainless-steel-sink grey. Some of English literature's most memorable scenes take place in summer. The party at Box Hill in Jane Austen's *Emma*, the opening of Laurie Lee's *Cider with Rosie*, every word of L. P. Hartley's *The Go-Between*; these books exploit every English native's yearning for days of sun and warmth.

What Thomas saw that summer's day is enriched and embroidered with what he heard. The final verse turns gloriously and evocatively to sound.

> *And for that minute a blackbird sang*
> *Close by, and round him, mistier,*
> *Farther and farther, all the birds*
> *Of Oxfordshire and Gloucestershire.*

This is where treating metrophobia becomes a daunting challenge. If you are unfamiliar with a blackbird's song, if you have never noticed or stopped just to listen to one, sitting on a fence or bush in front of you in spring or early summer, on your way home from school or trudging back from some suburban railway station, it is almost impossible to appreciate how uplifting it is to hear that burst of variety in their song, the sudden shooting to a higher note. They sing way above their weight. And of course blackbirds, like other birds, respond to each others' calls and Thomas hears these birds singing, farther and farther away; *mistier*, an ingenious way to convey the idea of a sound growing more and more indistinct in the distance, and an equally ingenious rhyme with the last syllable of *Gloucestershire*.

Finally, Thomas sings himself, as it were, producing a concise last line as mellifluous and delightful as the song of a blackbird, *Of Oxfordshire and Gloucestershire*. Imagine that being read by a really poor reader, the kind who mumbles and pauses because they have never mastered punctuation, or by anyone who is just learning English. Like so much of our mother tongue, it demands care and attention to detail, an ability to pronounce curious combinations of letters clearly and with confidence, *sheer* when it looks like *shire* and *gloss* instead of *glou*, as in *glue*. Thomas actually uses sound to draw our attention to our own rich dialects and history.

You can begin to see why this apparently slight and simple little poem captures so much of what it means to be English. Thomas is generally known as a war poet, not because he wrote much in the way of poetry about the Great War, like others who bear that ill-fated label. But because he was one of the most ill-fated ones. He is buried in Row C, grave number 43, at the

Commonwealth War Graves cemetery at Agny, in France. He was thirty-seven years old, married, with a son and two daughters, when he joined up, which at the time meant he would not be conscripted to fight, yet he chose to became a soldier nonetheless in the summer of 1915. In the spring, on Easter Monday two years later, a bullet went straight through his chest on the first day of the Battle of Arras, a battle that then went on to destroy another 285,000 men from opposing sides.

War poetry has had its own shelf in the library for a long time now, not because it is inherently more beautiful, inspiring or even instructive than other historical poetic genres, but because it is so brutal, shocking and pitiful that we all hope that it might just get through to some of the most belligerent voices in our society whenever, as they periodically do, they are raised yet again. We are living through one of those periods right now.

The Point of Poetry is not as ambitious. It doesn't set out to change the world. It just seeks to encourage readers reluctant to engage with it that poetry is there to be enjoyed and valued. This is not something pandas, llamas or cuttlefish get to share. Poetry is a uniquely human birthright.

Thomas never saw any of his poetry published and everything about his story underscores the calamitous waste of talent and scale of human loss that particular war demanded of the nation. Almost a hundred years after he was shot dead, that sense of loss was still searing enough for over 5 million ordinary people to feel the need to visit the strange sight of a sea of 888,246 ceramic poppies flowing around the Tower of London, representing the death of 888,246 British and Colonial soldiers between 1914 and 1918. The numbers, like Thomas's poem, bear repeating.

The Great War was a terrible turning point in English history. One of those moments when the seesaw every life teeters on, even that of a whole nation, dropped suddenly and without warning. It took a long time to lift again and rebalance. Unassuming little 'Adlestrop' is a vivid snapshot of the innocent joy we like to believe preceded this national catastrophe, a portrait of the nation itself at its greatest, framed golden in verse. The Industrial Revolution had stopped revolting, our empire was the biggest the world had ever seen, and everyone in it knew their place. There is a fantasy harmony, calm and human warmth about that period in the nation's past, which we populate with rolling green fields, cricket matches and parasols instead of umbrellas. 'Adlestrop' is it.

Adlestrop

Yes. I remember Adlestrop—
The name, because one afternoon
Of heat the express-train drew up there
Unwontedly. It was late June.

The steam hissed. Someone cleared his throat.
No one left and no one came
On the bare platform. What I saw
Was Adlestrop—only the name

And willows, willow-herb, and grass,
And meadowsweet, and haycocks dry,
No whit less still and lonely fair
Than the high cloudlets in the sky.

And for that minute a blackbird sang
Close by, and round him, mistier,
Farther and farther, all the birds
Of Oxfordshire and Gloucestershire.

Six

Break of Day in the Trenches
(1916)
Isaac Rosenberg (1890–1918)

Third from bottom of sixteen white names painted on dark grey slate in Westminster Abbey's Poets' Corner is one of the lucky ones who outlasted the war, Siegfried Sassoon (1886–1967). Sassoon made it out more or less in one piece, although his increasingly strident anger at what he witnessed and experienced in the trenches persuaded his seniors to send him to Craiglockhart military psychiatric hospital. They declared him unfit for service, after a letter he had written, condemning what was going on, was read out in the House of Commons. Sassoon was admired as an officer, far more by the squaddies he led than senior officers, and earned a reputation for reckless courage, as well as the Military Cross, awarded after he spent an hour and a half under fire, bringing in dead and wounded men. I memorised his poem 'The General' as a student, and can still recite it today. It expresses succinctly what the entire nation soon came to believe about the way that war was conducted.

> '*Good-morning, good-morning!*' *the General said*
> *When we met him last week on our way to the line.*
> *Now the soldiers he smiled at are most of 'em dead,*
> *And we're cursing his staff for incompetent swine.*
> '*He's a cheery old card,*' *grunted Harry to Jack*
> *As they slogged up to Arras with rifle and pack.*
>
> *But he did for them both by his plan of attack.*

Curving around the sixteen white names in Poets' Corner, in contrasting red, are these few words by Sassoon's friend, Wilfred Owen, killed in 1918, a week before the war ended, arguably the most famous war poet: *My subject is war, and the pity of war. The poetry is in the pity.* But directly above Sassoon's name is the less well-known name Isaac Rosenberg. I want to focus this chapter on Rosenberg's wonderful and painterly 'Break of Day in the Trenches'.

How much this single poem or John McCrae's poem, 'In Flanders Fields', contributed to anchoring the poppy as a symbol of soldierly sacrifice across Europe is impossible to gauge, because the connection between these startlingly scarlet flowers and the fragility of life on the battlefield sinks deep roots in our shared history, but no one has used that symbol in poetry more poignantly than Rosenberg.

There are no characters in 'Break of Day in the Trenches', unless you include the *queer, sardonic rat* that *leaps* Rosenberg's hand, where he waits in a French trench at dawn. He calls it

Droll later and enjoys a little, one-sided, imaginary conversation with it, marvelling at its freedom to move between the opposing sides, *To cross the sleeping green between.* He even cracks a bitter joke, *Droll rat, they would shoot you if they knew/Your cosmopolitan sympathies.* Observing the way it moves so close to men, unafraid, Rosenberg is baffled at the immensity of the role reversal. A creature regarded in any civilised city as vermin is elevated above man in *The torn fields of France*. He imagines the rat gets *pleasure* from its freedom of movement, and wonders what it is thinking about the hundreds of men it passes in the trenches. *It seems you inwardly grin*, he thinks, at the sight of *Strong eyes, fine limbs, haughty athletes,* constantly facing death *Sprawled in the bowels of the earth* and feeling far more vulnerable in this terrible place than the rat. That *grin* suggests the rat too knows the status quo has changed, and is even amused.

It is deeply disturbing to reflect on the reality that this particular war valued the lives of hundreds of thousands of free men less than a rat's. The one Rosenberg saw almost certainly reached the trenches with its furry chums on some military transport, but at the time, Londoners like Rosenberg, familiar with the East End of the city, would have known that beneath the streets there was an army of these disease-carrying, unpleasant rodents, mostly out of sight and mind. There is a popular urban myth even today that in a city, you are never more than six feet away from a rat, and I've certainly seen dozens of them partying on the pavement in Lincoln's Inn in the twilight, but the reality is, of course, very different. Where I live you're far more likely to be mugged by a squirrel used to packing its cheeks full of nuts stolen from suburban bird tables than by a sewer-dwelling rodent.

Myth or no myth, the dramatic change of fortunes is what matters here. A lousy uniform, especially literally, is not enough to civilise anyone. Rosenberg wrote quite a funny, macabre poem called 'Louse Hunting' about soldiers struggling to deal with more intimate vermin.

Rosenberg appears to be alone in 'Break of Day in the Trenches'. He doesn't mention friends or comrades, and the poem's dawn setting, *The darkness crumbles away*, reinforces the sense we have of him standing alone in the trench, *As I pull the parapet's poppy*. That picking of the frail, scarlet flower *To stick behind my ear* is so obviously the act of an artist. Rosenberg, like Blake, started out as an engraver's apprentice, but then went on to study painting at the Slade School of Fine Art, and some of his paintings are exhibited in Tate Britain, the National Portrait Gallery and the Imperial War Museum. He vacillated between the two art forms, but letters he wrote in France show that he opted finally for poetry.

Ironically, one of the most distinctive things about 'Break of Day in the Trenches' is that it looks and sounds like the work of a painter. The beautiful and pitiful idea, *Poppies whose roots are in man's veins*, which brings the poem to a close, is precisely the kind of image a strong, visual mind would turn to. That's the kind of intertwining of human and vegetable limbs Blake would have loved. It also gives me an opportunity to do a bit of metrophobic first aid. Ask yourself why Rosenberg uses *man's* and not *men's* in that image? You might be surprised, but changing just that one letter makes a dramatic difference. Poetry is a highly disciplined intellectual exercise. You are forced by things like rhyme and rhythm, or even just by the shape of the poem on the written page, to think hard and carefully about the words and sounds you choose. For example, a ballad, which is made up of four lines in every verse, with rhymes that alternate, constrains you in a way unrhymed blank verse does not.

Men's would be what a schoolboy poet opts for. It makes the connection between the soldiers dying in the mud of the trenches and the red flowers direct and obvious. It's easy to conjure up the consequent image, as in some 1960s anti-war propaganda poster. But *man's*, as in mankind, is a far more powerful, provocative concept. It acknowledges that, however terrible and horrifying the soldier's predicament, that morning, that moment as he stands there alone, silently contemplating the awfulness of his situation, he is just one of many millions of ordinary men over the ages who have found themselves innocently embroiled in war. Unlike many of the other war poets, who were well-educated officers, Rosenberg was a poorly educated squaddie, and not a very good one. He had a bad chest, was just over five feet tall, which meant he was placed in a Bantam unit (for men under five feet three inches) and in many respects he was the opposite of Sassoon: disorganised, untidy and forgetful. Not the best attributes for anyone in the military.

Rosenberg suffered from bronchitis so badly that after he left the Slade, a Jewish charity paid for his fare to Cape Town where his sister Mina lived, in the hope his health might improve. When it did, he came back to England, aiming to pursue a career as a painter. Failing to find work, he joined the army in 1915 in a mood more of resignation than anything else, and asked that half his salary go directly to his mother. Rosenberg was no naïve patriot. He didn't join the army to fight for king and country, Uncle Sam or to kill the Hun. In a letter he wrote at the time he said, 'I suppose we must all fight to get the trouble over.'

There are more than a few moments in this poem that bring Blake to mind, even specifically 'The Tyger'. That quick-fire trio of 'what' questions, *What do you see in our eyes . . . What quaver—what heart aghast?* could so easily be Blake. Their incompleteness, the paring down of the whole into just the *What quaver* and *what heart aghast?*, which means the reader, you and I, have to supply the rest if we're going to understand the full question, is also typical Blake. Poetry is so often parsimonious. It makes us work for our supper. As if to underscore the Blake connection, *At the shrieking iron and flame/Hurled through still heavens?* are two lines any mischievous editor could so easily transplant into almost any poem by Blake and get away scot-free because no one would notice. Blake loved a bit of flaming metal shrieking through the heavens. I'm only surprised there is no colourful self-portrait of him, spear in one hand, golden bow in the other, reins between his teeth, driving a chariot of fire between unfolding clouds, wearing Noddy's hat.

Polluting Rosenberg with Blake might be amusing, but it runs the risk of overshadowing the beauty and originality of his own poem. Those two characteristics come together in the last four lines when he turns again to the poppies for inspiration and comfort. Rooted in human blood, like the soldiers surrounding him they are equally short-lived, they *Drop, and are ever dropping*, the verb used by any amateur gardener to describe the annoying habit some flowers have of losing their petals, and their beauty, far too quickly. Try substituting the correct, scientific term 'abscise' just to get some sense of why poets are so choosy. Rosenberg's withering war poem ends, *But mine in my ear is safe,/ Just a little white with the dust.* The white dust reminds him of his own mortality, that he is safe for now, while reminding us of those tragic fields planted so tidily with white headstones. How sad that he wasn't even granted the dignity of being under one of them.

There are different accounts of his death. He had been assigned to a unit transporting barbed wire but was caught up in an unexpected German counter-attack at night during the battle of Arras, close to a village called Fampoux, and died on 1 April 1918. He was buried in a mass grave but later reinterred and given his own headstone, although the exhumation report on the Commonwealth War Graves Commission's website linked to Rosenberg describes the reinterred body as being 'well-developed' and between five feet nine and ten inches tall.

I'm writing this a few days after thousands of parents and young children thought they were safe at a concert in Manchester city centre. At the moment twenty-two are dead and fifty-nine injured, but I've no doubt by the time you come to read this, those numbers will have shifted tragically, together with the lives of all those who knew them. They died in precisely the same way hundreds of thousands of the Great War's victims died, shattered by fragments of hot metal in an explosion triggered by another human being specifically to kill them. An outpouring of public grief immediately followed that would have been unthinkable when Rosenberg stood in his trench and picked up that poppy.

When Britain went to war in 1914 it handed out white feathers to conscientious objectors with one hand, while thrusting food parcels into the hands of departing volunteers with the other, all with the confidence due its vast empire. But as the numbers and corpses piled up unimaginably, that confidence was tested to breaking point. That Manchester city centre could hold thousands, genuinely mourning a few dozen children they never knew, is in part possible because of the scale of what happened to Rosenberg's entire generation. The poet Laurence Binyon wrote about their legacy in his 1914 poem 'For the Fallen', and it is because as a nation we do indeed still *remember them* that all subsequent attacks on us, as a nation, provoke such strength of feeling.

The Manchester attack took place in the middle of a general election and shortly before it, my youngest daughter came home bubbling and beaming with pleasure about a mock election her school had held during the day. It wasn't the mock election or the speeches pupils made which she was energised about, funny and entertaining though they clearly were, it was the lengthy conversation she had had with a group of girls afterwards, in private, which she spoke about so fondly and enthusiastically. No one bickered, no one resorted to dogma or emotion and, crucially, no one took offence. Yet she found what they had to say fascinating and even exciting. It was 'a really good day' at school.

Many reading this might connect her pleasure with their own teenage or student years when, unshackled by preconception, prejudice or predisposition, they listened and shared ideas freely, respectfully and with unadulterated, academic delight. The terrorist who killed children in Manchester was born in the city and educated there. So I find myself asking, not whether or not he had been taught any war poetry, but how many of those 'really good' days at school he had.

Those who went to Manchester city centre for an evening vigil listened to a number of speakers, local and national politicians, but they also heard a local poet, Tony Walsh, read one of his poems. They listened, they understood, and they cheered. The internet lapped Walsh's verse up greedily and many hundreds of thousands of people living in cities as different from Manchester as one could imagine will have heard it too. So here's a question for any metrophobe who has got this far but is still unconvinced. Why was that? Why, of all the various ways feelings can be expressed did so many ordinary people, people who would never dream of reading a poem at home alone, respond to one at a time of such extremity and grief? Why is there a special corner of Westminster Abbey reserved not for bankers or footballers, celebrities or film stars, or even orators and essayists? There's no special corner even for politicians, although no doubt we could all find one. Why, as a nation, do we save such a sacred space for poets?

Break of Day in the Trenches

The darkness crumbles away.
It is the same old druid Time as ever,
Only a live thing leaps my hand,
A queer sardonic rat,
As I pull the parapet's poppy
To stick behind my ear.
Droll rat, they would shoot you if they knew
Your cosmopolitan sympathies.
Now you have touched this English hand
You will do the same to a German
Soon, no doubt, if it be your pleasure
To cross the sleeping green between.
It seems you inwardly grin as you pass
Strong eyes, fine limbs, haughty athletes,
Less chanced than you for life,
Bonds to the whims of murder,
Sprawled in the bowels of the earth,
The torn fields of France.
What do you see in our eyes
At the shrieking iron and flame
Hurled through still heavens?
What quaver—what heart aghast?
Poppies whose roots are in man's veins
Drop, and are ever dropping;
But mine in my ear is safe—
Just a little white with the dust.

Seven

When I am dead, my dearest
(1862)
Christina Rossetti (1830–1894)

One of the very easiest things to spot when you get interested in the art and craft of poetry is similarity. What else is a rhyme but two words with similar sound? What else is rhythm but two lines that follow the same beat? The preferred title of this 'Song', by the Victorian poet Christina Rossetti, 'When I am dead, my dearest', is an example. There are only two strong words in it. Strong because of the hard 'd' sound they begin with (the stress that naturally falls on those syllables), because it is quickly repeated, and because you can actually see the same pattern at the start of those words, *dead* and *dearest*. If you still struggle with the idea of natural stress in words, just think of emphasis instead and read this: **su**per**cali***frag*ilistic***exp***ialli***doc***ious. Now try and read it unnaturally, by stressing the syllables that aren't italicised. Next, read the first line of Rossetti's poem and stress the last syllable, *When I am dead, my dear***est***. Sound a bit like a French speaker talking about 'Great Britane' as in 'Gitanes'? Now you know all about stressed and unstressed syllables.

I often think one of the dropped passes lots of metrophobes must have received were from teachers who put considerable effort into rhyme and rhythm, maybe even stress and that formal term, metre, but who never told them to *look* at a poem, at how it *looks* on the page. Add to that the idea that the second syllable of dea*rest* is synonymous with death and that *my* is aurally almost a perfect reversal of *I am,* and you will begin to appreciate just how condensed, intense and skilful poetry is when you start to learn how to read and admire it. As you develop an ear and an eye for it, balance and harmony will gain your attention long before you learn to dwell on the ideas the words convey.

We've met Christina's famous brother, Dante Gabriel Rossetti before, in chapter four. Besides using William Morris's wife as a model, he also used his sister and she sat for two of his early paintings, *The Girlhood of Mary Virgin*, his first full painting in oils and the first to be signed with the PRB monogram that signified the Pre-Raphaelite Brotherhood, and *Ecce Ancilla Domini!* (*The Annunciation*), which he painted the following year. Both were painted in 1849–50, when Christina was nineteen years old. She had already successfully published some poetry: the Rossetti family was nothing if not talented, and if you want to see what she really looked like, then the Getty Image library contains several early black-and-white photographs, as well as a range of drawings and sketches of her, although all of them seem to suffer from the same inordinate desire to portray a living saint. She actually is a real Anglican saint, although to be specific, a *heroine*, because after the Reformation the Church of England had a bit of an issue with the whole concept of saintliness. The execution of Charles I, most especially his saintly performance when the curtain finally came down on his head, gave the Church, as well as Charles, a serious migraine and some Anglicans still think of him as that particularly overzealous kind of saint, a martyr. In the end, the Church finally opted for the less controversial notion of heroes and heroines instead at the Lambeth Conference in 1958.

There are a few writers and poets hiding in the catalogue of Anglican heroes and heroines today. They include, unsurprisingly, John Donne and George Herbert but rather more surprisingly, since he is generally thought of as just the dictionary guy, Samuel Johnson. Christina's feast day is 27 April, which in the Catholic Church she shares with the splendidly named St Liberalis of Treviso and St Floribert of Liege, amongst others. Study Christina Rossetti's life and I suspect you'll conclude, as I have, that paradoxically, she would have rather liked that.

Christina was an extremely religious child, teenager and woman. She wrote arguably as much about Christianity as anything else and was deeply caught up in the Oxford Movement of the mid-Victorian era, which saw the dominant Anglican church succumb to the dreaded influence of Catholicism for the first time since Henry VIII listed lust under the Divine Right of Kings. She spent an awful lot of time in church, which, when linked with her rejection of at least two suitors for religious reasons, one apparently because of his preference for Catholicism, and another because he was agnostic (talk about choosy), has unleashed a whole world of painfully solipsistic literary criticism.

She has that kind of star status bookish teens normally reserve for unrealised talent that dies young, only she made it to sixty-four before breast cancer caught up with her. The empathy teenage girls with a literary sensibility given to bouts of self-doubt might feel for her today is perhaps not all that misplaced. According to her biography from the Poetry Foundation,[1] she told a niece in her later years:

> *You must not imagine, my dear girl, that your Aunt was always the calm and sedate person you now behold. I, too, had a very passionate temper; but I learnt to control it. On one occasion, being rebuked by my dear Mother for some fault, I seized upon a pair of scissors, and ripped up my arm to vent my wrath. I have learnt since to control my feelings – and no doubt you will!*

That she remained unmarried yet produced poetry as a young girl that is full of passionate feeling is sufficient reason for some to seek and find every imaginable kind of Freudian secret lurking in her verse. Her close association with Pre-Raphaelite artists who could barely paint any female form without urging you to undress it doesn't help. 'When I am dead, my dearest' is typical of the kind of poem she produced, which provokes such wild variation in interpretation amongst fans.

It's a little like a true ballad in form but strays far enough away to break the tie, which is possibly why so many of the versions of it put to music are so awful. If you doubt me, just spend half an hour on YouTube. It's easy and tempting to read it as from a young woman to her lover, the romantic failsafe for anyone seduced by the image of a lovely and lonely teenage girl, waiting to be swept off the floor she has probably hurled herself onto in a fit of grief brought on by the sight of a fox lunching on her pet kitten. But the sex of the speaker is deliberately unclear and that lack of clarity is one of the poem's defining characteristics. Rossetti deliberately avoids certainty throughout. I enjoy that in any poem. It makes you think.

The lines are short and there are only two verses, each only eight lines long. It is a deceptively simple little song. To make things easier let's assume, as the majority of commentators do, that the poet's voice is indeed young and female. The Victorians made a real song and dance about death. We forget that. We live in a world where lurid tinsel windmills spin jauntily above graves side by side with fat, gas-filled balloons spelling out 'Gran'. I used to live close to a graveyard. My two daughters learned to ride their bikes there. I can recommend it to young parents. Cemeteries are perfect test beds for little pedallers. Lots of narrow, smooth, empty paths, thoughtfully surrounded by soft grass to catch them when they fall off laughing. I was as often moved to laughter by the things I found decorating fresh graves. I was especially entertained one day by the lovingly inscribed packet of cigarettes wrapped in cling film someone had placed centre stage on a freshly dug mound of earth, next to a small pyramid of empty cans of lager.

Directly rejecting the conventions of the age, when widows still wore black and you could pay wan children to walk tearfully behind your hearse, itself led by glossy black horses sporting even glossier black ostrich plumes, she tells her beloved immediately not to mourn her, *Sing no sad songs for me;/Plant thou no roses at my head,* but *Be the green grass above me.* That *Be* is an absolute gem. It's so unexpected. How can anyone *be* grass? I hope by now you can *see* the way it connects with *green*, never mind the obvious alliteration between *green* and *grass*. Identifying any poetic technique, such as alliteration – which at its simplest is just the repetition of syllable sounds – might show that you know about poetic techniques, but what use is that? It's always what lies behind the use of the technique that matters. There are, of course, poets who use technique consciously and to show off, but the best can, and do, much better. 'Green grass' is a cliché, and whatever else you recall from school, you probably remember being told to avoid clichés . . . like the plague, or at least like getting into the back of a cab with Donald Trump. Why would a poet of Rossetti's talent chose something as obvious? Well, the line that precedes that grassy one is, *Nor shady cypress tree*, which places the word *cypress* directly above *grass*. Am I going too slowly for you?

Green is the only colour mentioned in the entire poem. There's no black, even the roses aren't red, and she doesn't *see the shadows* in the last verse. That *green grass* is there not just because of the sound it makes but because *green* is young and vital, a symbol of youth and inexperience, in perfect harmony with the impression created of this poem being about a young life lost. The next line of interest I'll just leave you to stare at and get on with, to see how the treatment plan is going. The *green grass* she imagines growing above her grave is *With showers and dewdrops wet*.

If I asked you to list words you'd expect to find in a Victorian poem about mourning it's a fair guess 'tears' would brim close, if not right to the top. Rossetti gives us *showers* and *dewdrops* instead. One of the things she loved in life was the natural world. Up to the age of nine she enjoyed long spells at her grandparents' home in Holmer Green, then a tiny hamlet in rural Buckinghamshire, and in a book written much later, she describes studying the natural world she found there with the kind of fine attention to detail we expect of intellectually curious children. In her late twenties she brought the same forensic habits to bear on the prostitutes she met as a volunteer working at the St Mary Magdalene Penitentiary in Highgate, a charity dedicated to the 'reclamation' of 'fallen' women. How lacking ambition are we? Our hi-tech, state of-the-art reclamation units handle bottles, cans and newspapers. The Victorians went for the soul.

She spent a lot of time at this institution after she had been rejected as a volunteer nurse for the Crimean War, and her poetry is freely populated with girls who are a little unsteady on their feet. The central theme of *Goblin Market*, one of her most famous individual poems and the title poem of her most successful collection, deals with two sisters, Laura and Lizzie, their moral rectitude and turpitude and opts for a very elaborate Victorian way, fairy tale, of posing a much simpler question about sexual maturity and choice. Such is the determination of modern critics and fans to find hidden Freudian secrets in Rossetti's verse, I'm not joking when I suggest there is almost certainly more than one postgraduate study gathering internet dust bytes that builds an entire edifice of sexual frustration around the possibility that 'Lizzie' is obviously a Freudian typo.

Which brings us more credibly back to the determination of 'When I am dead, my dearest' to evade certainty. We've assumed it is the voice of a young girl, but Rossetti deliberately ignores the speaker's gender, a decision that forces us to think a little more than we might otherwise. Uncertainty is the crux of this poem. The first verse ends with these two ingeniously indecisive lines, *And if thou wilt, remember,/And if thou wilt, forget.* Even though I can embrace the way she generously frees the one left behind from any responsibility to grieve, I can't shake off that repetitive insistence on *wilt*, caused by rhythm and punctuation that places a clear and forceful pause after each use of the word. If you think you're developing an appetite for poetic terminology, this kind of pause in the middle of any line of poetry is called a caesura.

The choice is for the living. She makes no demands, but *thou wilt* was an archaic choice of words even for a Victorian and poets are never so dangerous as when they choose unusual words, when obvious ones come straight to mind. Dead flowers of course, wilt.

Critics often refer to a poem's tone because it's a helpful concept. Identifying tone and being able to describe it moves us closer to understanding. The tone of Rossetti's poem is especially intriguing. It's worth acknowledging that Rossetti didn't invent this type of poem, written to a loved one anticipating their reaction to your own death. These range from the childish, emotional blackmail of the 'you'll be sorry when I'm gone' school of verse, to the profoundly sincere. Something like John Donne's 'A Valediction Forbidding Mourning', which is immaculate love poetry. (A valediction is simply a kind of farewell.) Rossetti's is neither because of the surprising tone it adopts. That tone is one of calm acceptance, a kind of gentle stoicism that celebrates life and love without fear of death.

In the second verse she turns from the live half of the couple to the dead half. In a repetitive burst of unequivocal statements beginning *I shall not*, the repetition underscores the sense of loss and therefore also of love. All she felt, heard and saw in life is now denied her. It's a measure of Rossetti's skill that the things she denies her speaker are not joyful, overtly pleasurable, or sensual delights. It's not the sun on her face she will miss, the touch of the beloved's hand on her skin or the sound of their, or any other voice: *shadows, rain* and the nightingale's song are singled out as the objects of denial.

It might be dull brown and plain, but the nightingale is an eye-catching bird to introduce into any poem because poetry, like all literature, can't ever escape its mythic roots. Mythically, the nightingale is the reincarnation of the Greek princess Philomena, who was raped by her brother-in-law King Tereus and turned into a nightingale by the gods after she and her sister, Procne, cooked and fed him his own son as revenge for the rape. Nice family. The nightingale's beautiful song has consequently become synonymous with sorrow, which is why Rossetti thinks of it singing, *as if in pain*, and why it has been so eagerly embraced as a symbol by feminist artists.

The uncertainty that has hummed in the background throughout the entire poem finds its voice in the kind of paradise

Rossetti creates for her dead soul, *And dreaming through the twilight/That doth not rise nor set*, she insists she may, or may not, remember anything. It would be a bleak prospect if it were certain. But the *dreaming*, the *twilight* and its stubborn insistence on not giving way to day or night, all contribute to a complete sense of paradisiacal doubt. Whatever faith she might profess and however energetically she exercised it, the poem's speaker hasn't a clue what awaits her in death. The poem's conclusion provides a wonderful example of why people admire Rossetti's skill as a poet. In the last two lines, *Haply I may remember,/And haply may forget*, she rubs our faces in the ambiguity like a custard pie. *Haply* is another archaic word that carries the sense of 'perhaps', but read even with perfect enunciation, it's impossible not to hear 'happily' simultaneously. Now that really is clever.

'When I am dead, my dearest' is not really the poem it purports to be. Imagine an abstract painting, all soft pastel colours but no distinct forms, put inside a hugely ornate, heavy golden picture frame or flowers by Georgia O'Keeffe stuck inside one of those ponderous gilt frames that surround a portrait of Charles II. It has the outside of one kind of poem but the guts of another. It was written when Rossetti was still only eighteen and she sets us up to expect something a young, bookish Victorian girl might wistfully write, at least one who hasn't yet been in love or in lust but is chomping at the bit a bit. But it takes us somewhere else completely: into a reflection on the value of love, of any feeling at all, in the face of life's brevity and the unknowable nature of the human soul. The sharpness of her wit is astounding for a teenager and you end up admiring the speaker, because she embraces her own doubt so fearlessly and with a wit that makes you smile at your own gullibility.

Christina Rossetti is one of those poets who rewards you when you sense something interesting about the person behind the poem. Literary criticism that tears apart a writer's life in order to 'explain' their work usually tells you more about the critic than the writer, but some writers' lives seem designed to be investigated, after the event, as it were. Rossetti's was one of those.

When I am dead, my dearest

When I am dead, my dearest,
Sing no sad songs for me;
Plant thou no roses at my head,
Nor shady cypress tree:
Be the green grass above me
With showers and dewdrops wet;
And if thou wilt, remember,
And if thou wilt, forget.

I shall not see the shadows,
I shall not feel the rain;
I shall not hear the nightingale
Sing on, as if in pain:
And dreaming through the twilight
That doth not rise nor set,
Haply I may remember,
And haply may forget.

Eight

Mrs Midas
(1999)
Carol Ann Duffy (1955–)

Carol Ann Duffy is the current Poet Laureate, which means she has a lot to live up to. I admire anyone who follows in the footsteps of Dryden, Wordsworth, John Betjeman or Ted Hughes. There's something wry and acid about much of her poetry that proves a healthy antidote to our belligerently intolerant era. Her poem 'Mrs Midas', in itself a tart joke, takes up the idea of what it would be like to be married to the mythical king whose touch turned everything to gold.

The setting she chooses is domestic and modern. Much of the humour in the poem comes from the clash between the mythical golden objects his touch transforms like thrones and goblets, and their modern equivalents, a toilet and a wine glass, but not all. It's unusual to find an English poem that actually makes you smile that isn't about weird creatures and that uses even weirder language. The roots planted by Edward Lear's Jumblies and Lewis Carroll's Jabberwock run deep and far, so today it's more likely to be Dr Seuss who people think of when it comes to the kind of poetry that raises a smile. Spike Milligan or Hilaire Belloc might figure too, but Hollywood hasn't yet reanimated the Ning Nang Nong or Matilda – at least the one who told lies.

Duffy's Mrs Midas is less fantastic, a likeable, poignant figure with a distinct sense of humour that gradually fails against the shocking reality of finding herself married to a man who really does have the Midas touch. It's that idea of touch that sinks her, and at the poem's end she is left wistfully recalling how their young love for each other was fuelled and enriched by it. *I miss most,* she complains, *even now, his hands, his warm hands on my skin, his touch.*

Ironically, his miraculous gift impoverishes him, and on the very first night after he transforms a pear from their garden to gold, *it sat in his palm, like a lightbulb. On,* and he performs the same trick on enough domestic items to fill a blue Ikea bag, he ends up sleeping alone. Mrs Midas locks herself, and the cat, in another room, equally ironically, *near petrified.* Duffy's poem almost drowns in its own irony. She takes special pleasure replaying that shocking trope about food suddenly being transformed to gold. His attempt to eat the corn on the cob she has cooked for supper ends with him *spitting out the teeth of the rich.* After banishing him to a caravan in the woods they own, when she visits she finds,

> . . . *Golden trout*
> *on the grass. One day, a hare hung from a larch,*
> *a beautiful lemon mistake.*

Presumably the remnants of her husband's failed attempts to feed himself. That image of the hare is simply beautiful, the kind of unalloyed genius one expects from a poet laureate. He is indeed *thin* and *delirious* when she sees him, presumably for the last time, since she describes his hearing voices from the god Pan on that occasion as *the last straw*, a plain, mundane object that is also strikingly golden.

Duffy even lifts the veil on the irony by spelling it out.

> *Do you know about gold?*
> *It feeds no one; aurum, soft, untarnishable; slakes*
> *no thirst.*

Which is where the fireworks really start for me. Such an easy thing to say when you have hard cash, so hard to swallow when you don't. Catch the poetry-reading bug, as I hope you will, and it won't be long before you realise there are poets who have designs on you. This book isn't an exploration of why poets write. There are clearly many different reasons. Accumulating gold, I would suggest, is rarely one of them, but a desire to convince you about something has to be right up there amongst the most common. Which means when you make that decision to read a poem, you should also be prepared to have your own views or opinions tested. It is one of poetry's greatest gifts, this invitation to hear others' creative, imaginative thoughts. But it necessarily means that there will be times when you disagree, when a poet's view collides head-on with your own. That might make you cross, frustrated, even angry, and the risk all poets take when they tread the convincing route is that you might reject them, as well as their ideas. My advice is to dig deeper into the poem, because the experience only becomes richer and more delightful. This is what digging looks like.

When Mrs Midas utters that rhetorical question, *Do you know about gold?* Whether she likes it or not, *gold* is a metonym, a word made to understudy another, in this case, money. When the pen is mightier than the sword (which probably explains why a lot of poets tread the convincing route) both *pen* and *sword* stand in for much larger concepts: the very act of writing or the art of war. Even a phrase as commonly used as 'the White House' is a metonym, because when people deploy it they are expecting you to imagine an entire, neoclassical building, humming with the combined brainpower of hundreds of skilled, intelligent professionals all focused on running the vast United States of America, and Donald Trump.

So Mrs Midas is using metonymy to express her repugnance for money, for material wealth. Yet simultaneously she confidently asserts, *It feeds no one. . . slakes no thirst.* Well, the last time I dumped the shopping basket at the checkout, the machine ate my fiver fairly greedily.

So I don't buy what Mrs Midas is selling. Gold, money, feeds families. It puts bread on the table and it keeps people safe (and if you spotted the metonym there you're a star, which is a mere metaphor). This doesn't mean I don't like Carol Ann Duffy's poem. In fact, it means she gives me something of considerable value. She makes me think for myself. And what she made me think about was Charles Dickens.

One of the things that has always baffled and irritated me as someone who has read Dickens and not just got by on *The Muppet Christmas Carol* is the way so many critical academic voices have subsumed his fiction on one side of that false equation: poverty = crime. Entire political parties buy into the great Dickensian lie. Young political activists retell it enthusiastically as though it's gospel, never once having appreciated the profound moral courage so many of Dickens's impoverished characters display under extreme duress. Crime is a moral choice for Dickens, as for so many truly great writers. Few novelists have mapped out the ingenuous journey it takes in such astounding detail and so insightfully. Jonas Chuzzlewit, Bradley Headstone, Daniel Quilp are like detective grad school case studies. For every criminal who stumbles and falls in Dickens, there is a small host of equally hard-done-by men and women, even children, who do not. They are saintly in their endurance and adamantine in their ethics. Yet this false equation between poverty and crime still gets replayed again and again on every possible media platform.

So one of the benefits of reading 'Mrs Midas', for me, is that it reminds me of other great literature I value and have learned something from. I now know at least one reason why I go back and reread Dickens so often. Because he helps me form my own views and make sense of the culture and society in which I have chosen to live.

Not being poverty-stricken means Midas's wife can accuse him of *greed* as well as *idiocy* before deciding it was his *pure selfishness* that finished her, his *lack of thought for me*. Now isn't that interesting? Not privy to his thinking or to any of the life that led her unfortunate husband to make his wish, we have to rely completely on our narrator's version of events. Fairy stories abound with examples of the nagging, greedy wife whose increasing scale of demands ruins her and her husband's lives. *The Fisherman and his Wife* is one of the best, and sees the wife go full circle from poverty to palatial excess and back to poverty in order to find what Mrs Midas loses, a loving husband.

Carol Ann Duffy features frequently on the exam syllabus and 'Mrs Midas' is one of the handful of poems thousands of schoolchildren encounter in their entire lives, even more of a burden than her laureateship. Classrooms will buzz with discussions about loneliness and greed, about the choices we make in life, and inevitably gender and relationships will figure strongly. A consensus will almost certainly settle like a comfortable cardi on the side of the neglected wife. Yet I can't help that nagging suspicion that this isn't the whole story. What we hear is just one side and once you think that, then it's a nanosecond before you also think, why? Time to dig again.

'Mrs Midas' is from a collection Duffy wrote called *The World's Wife* in which she takes famous characters from fairy tales and literature she loved as a child, those memorable characters she had been taught about at school and who, in her own words:

> *had formed my imagination as a writer. I wanted to retell these very familiar stories and characters, in the way that Shakespeare demonstrates a writer should do, perhaps to find something hidden or surprising in the familiar, or simply to celebrate and sometimes to subvert and annoy people.*

It's understandable and indeed clever that she chooses to do this by adopting the voices of these characters' wives. But read other poems from the same collection, 'Mrs Tiresias', 'Mrs Faust' or 'Mrs Aesop', for example, and an unmistakable pattern starts to emerge, a pattern that makes you question the disingenuousness of the project. What connects these women is far more noticeable than what surprises.

As wives they are dismal failures. They snip the Gordian marriage knot with kitchen scissors. It's a chillingly non-familial image of the family they advocate, for all their brooding on children. Duffy's clever reversal of roles is a game anyone can play. The world of literature and poetry, dominated as it is historically by male writers, is consequently never short of female interest. I for one would love to read 'The Husband of Bath' or 'Ophelia, Princess of Denmark'. I considered 'Lady Macbeth' but, as I said, it's a game anyone can play and Shakespeare's done that one already.

Researching this essay I found a video online of Carol Ann Duffy performing 'Mrs Midas' at an event held at an Oxford Street department store. Early in my writing career I wrote a play in which a character joked about the direction theatre was taking and how it wouldn't be long before productions of *Macbeth* were sponsored by the makers of kitchen knives, or *Othello* by manufacturers of pillows. I struggled to find the department-store connection in this particular case, although wine and mince pies did seem to figure somewhere.

I discussed the value or not of poets reading their own work in chapter two on George Mackay Brown. But watching her read 'Mrs Midas' and other poems, I was strangely drawn not to Carol Ann Duffy's voice or reading, but to the audience and especially their reactions. The producers had decided they were an important component of the whole event, so the camera panned languidly across faces glued to the lectern, resting occasionally for a close-up on someone especially rapt or studiedly amused. The average age was about twenty-three and my sincere sympathy, which had moved me to write this book for the disarmed army of metrophobes out there, recognised something of real importance. No wonder, I thought, so many of you feel excluded. Here was a clique in all its self-contained, *don't call us: we'll call you,* exclusivity. I recognised it easily because my earliest encounters with contemporary poetry, as a student in London in the late seventies, demonstrated this repeatedly. So often what I found myself outside of, in those darkened backstairs rooms or cluttered bookshops, even in the place where I studied, was a clique.

Listening to a radio broadcast more recently, about the popularity of poetry on Instagram, I heard an academic comment on how so many ordinary people felt excluded from poetry in the same way they did from opera. He argued that Instagram's closed world allowed people to respond more freely and honestly, to enjoy what they liked most. I think he's right about that.

Smug is just too short and too slight a word to describe the mood that lit up one face after another in the video like a contagious yawn. For someone like me, who enjoys poetry like Duffy's, watching this video was a disturbing experience. I imagine a Scientology Thanksgiving dinner looks very similar. Superiority oozed from every pore like invisible sweat as audience members competed with each other over who got the jokes quickest or best. The men joined in, displaying such abject obeisance I can only imagine they were all fishermen. I've seen the poetry clique exert its quiet, superior authority on numerous occasions in live events and online publishing has only emboldened it. It's not something poets, or fans of poetry, should be proud of.

It's hard breaking a clique down. It's easier to rise above it, so if you find yourself being made to feel an outsider or interloper, not one of the select literati, dig deep. Focus on the salad and ignore the dressing.

Mrs Midas

It was late September. I'd just poured a glass of wine, begun
to unwind, while the vegetables cooked. The kitchen
filled with the smell of itself, relaxed, its steamy breath
gently blanching the windows. So I opened one,
then with my fingers wiped the other's glass like a brow.
He was standing under the pear tree snapping a twig.

Now the garden was long and the visibility poor, the way
the dark of the ground seems to drink the light of the sky,
but that twig in his hand was gold. And then he plucked
a pear from a branch. – we grew Fondante d'Automne –
and it sat in his palm, like a lightbulb. On.
I thought to myself, Is he putting fairy lights in the tree?

He came into the house. The doorknobs gleamed.
He drew the blinds. You know the mind; I thought of
the Field of the Cloth of Gold and of Miss Macready.
He sat in that chair like a king on a burnished throne.
The look on his face was strange, wild, vain. I said,
What in the name of God is going on? He started to laugh.

I served up the meal. For starters, corn on the cob.
Within seconds he was spitting out the teeth of the rich.
He toyed with his spoon, then mine, then with the knives,
   the forks.

He asked where was the wine. I poured with a shaking
    hand,
a fragrant, bone-dry white from Italy, then watched
as he picked up the glass, goblet, golden chalice, drank.

It was then that I started to scream. He sank to his
    knees.
After we'd both calmed down, I finished the wine
on my own, hearing him out. I made him sit
on the other side of the room and keep his hands to
    himself.
I locked the cat in the cellar. I moved the phone.
The toilet I didn't mind. I couldn't believe my ears:

how he'd had a wish. Look, we all have wishes; granted.
But who has wishes granted? Him. Do you know about
    gold?
It feeds no one; aurum, soft, untarnishable; slakes
no thirst. He tried to light a cigarette; I gazed, entranced,
as the blue flame played on its luteous stem. At least,
I said, you'll be able to give up smoking for good.

Separate beds. in fact, I put a chair against my door,
near petrified. He was below, turning the spare room
into the tomb of Tutankhamun. You see, we were
    passionate then,
in those halcyon days; unwrapping each other, rapidly,

like presents, fast food. But now I feared his honeyed
    embrace,
the kiss that would turn my lips to a work of art.

And who, when it comes to the crunch, can live
with a heart of gold? That night, I dreamt I bore
his child, its perfect ore limbs, its little tongue
like a precious latch, its amber eyes
holding their pupils like flies. My dream milk
burned in my breasts. I woke to the streaming sun.

So he had to move out. We'd a caravan
in the wilds, in a glade of its own. I drove him up
under the cover of dark. He sat in the back.
And then I came home, the woman who married the fool
who wished for gold. At first, I visited, odd times,
parking the car a good way off, then walking.

You knew you were getting close. Golden trout
on the grass. One day, a hare hung from a larch,
a beautiful lemon mistake. And then his footprints,
glistening next to the river's path. He was thin,
delirious; hearing, he said, the music of Pan
from the woods. Listen. That was the last straw.

What gets me now is not the idiocy or greed
but lack of thought for me. Pure selfishness. I sold
the contents of the house and came down here.

I think of him in certain lights, dawn, late afternoon, and once a bowl of apples stopped me dead. I miss most, even now, his hands, his warm hands on my skin, his touch.

Nine

Tractor
(1957)
Ted Hughes (1930–1998)

Poets find inspiration in the simplest of objects. Although that implies somehow that the beauty or interest was hiding in there somewhere, waiting to be found, like the story about the little boy who asks Michelangelo how he knew that man was inside the block of marble. John Donne infamously starts with a flea, *Mark but this flea*, and our old friend Blake sighs, *Ah Sun-flower!* at the start of a poem called, evidently with divine, pre-Impressionist inspiration, 'Ah! Sun-flower'.

There is nothing too mundane for a poet to think about, and the next poem I want to introduce, or perhaps reintroduce you too is 'Tractor' by Ted Hughes. It's another favourite with English teachers, so apologies if it's bored you before. That's a risk I'm willing to take, given the potential rewards.

Hughes was Poet Laureate from 1984 to 1998 and 'Tractor' was written in the seventies, so from the outset it's worth having some idea of what kind of machine he is writing about. His tractor is not some air-conditioned Goliath guided in a perfectly straight line across a vast space of brown earth by satellite. Hughes was brought up in that rural backbone of England, the Pennines, before the Second World War, and later in life he owned and managed a small farm in Devon. The blood of centuries of Englishmen who have lived and worked on the land pumps through his poetry. The physical, natural make-up of Eng*land*, and our day-to-day relationship with that last syllable, the way we rely on it for food and shelter, the animals and plants we share it with, always fascinated and engaged him. He is in essence a yeoman poet. 'Tractor' describes a man stepping out into the teeth of a winter's day so fiercely cold, it's as though he is being physically tortured.

His first job is to start his tractor. This is definitely one of those no-frills tractors, the kind with just a bare metal seat for the driver, two large wheels at the back and two smaller ones at the front. This machine has entrails which tells us it is one with its engine visible, the guts of the machine open to the air. In the face of this bitter winter's day, in weather Hughes strikingly describes as *head-pincering*, he attempts to get it started. The whole poem is devoted to that simple little action. An act he must have carried out hundreds of times, routinely and in all weathers. Yet in 'Tractor' it becomes a battle of flesh and will. Nothing is too mean or simple for a skilled poet.

I lived right at the southern tip of the Pennines for over a decade and remember vividly a January day I drove onto a moor to rough shoot with my springer spaniel, Jake. I walked to the back of the Land Rover, unhitched the tailgate and Jake sprang out as he always did, bursting with enthusiasm and, considering the quality of my marksmanship, a distinct degree of faithful canine optimism. Watching a spaniel look at you after you've missed a pheasant they have just worked so hard to find is a levelling experience I can recommend. Someone should bottle it for one of those TV charity ads designed to make you feel so guilty you stump up wads of cash for starving ponies, emaciated puppies or goldfish with dementia. The wind was so strong and steady I had to lean into it, squinting. Sleet came at me sideways in a biting, constant stream that didn't abate for one second. The only time I've ever felt colder was walking the streets of Novgorod, Russia, in December 1990, trying to find a brand new Austrian hotel, because that was the only place in the city where you could get a drink that wasn't Georgian white wine or that sugary excuse for a soft drink, *sok*.

Jake sat on his haunches and looked up at me as I pulled my shotgun out of its bag. When I turned into the sleet to view the ground, he tipped his head sideways, then jumped straight onto the open tailgate and back under the canvas shelter provided by the Land Rover. I looked at him and he looked back, and without exchanging a word we both knew his was the right decision. I wrapped him up in the thick towelling bag I used to dry him, returned my gun and the tailgate, then got back inside the front of the Land Rover, thankful my dog had more sense than me. And this was a dog who once retrieved a duck from the River Dove then sat quietly beside me in the failing light, hoping for more action, until I reached down as it grew darker to pat him and found his entire coat encrusted with ice. On another occasion, in another Pennine winter, I walked past the same Land

Rover to see its long aerial cocooned thick as my wrist in snow, whipping around in the wind. Worried the wind might snap it, I reached out to knock the snow off, only to find it was a single pole of solid ice. Winter is unpredictable in that part of the world.

Part of every poet's gift is unpredictability. They continually surprise us. 'Tractor' is full of surprises. Some of them are admirable examples of a figure of speech that is inherently elusive, the oxymoron. An oxymoron is simply an apparent contradiction that is in some, insightful way, not contradictory at all. It's most commonly created in verse by linking two opposite words directly together, and the effect it has on you varies from mere amusement to inspired astonishment. Long weekend, or tight slacks are examples of the former. At the other end of the scale, John Milton gave us *darkness visible* in *Paradise Lost* and Shakespeare's Sonnet 40 uses the phrase *lascivious grace*. Hughes gives us a number of these, which he yokes together to develop the central oxymoron that concludes the second verse, of the tractor being caught up in *its hell of ice*. When he first sees it, the tractor is *an agony* to contemplate, and *agony* is a word ringing with religious connotations connected with hell and damnation.

The best oxymorons make you think, 'Of course, that is absolutely true', and force you to reconsider something or look at it in a new light. They are often a way for a poet to characterise someone or something, or to surprise the reader with a new thought or idea. In a sense the entire first verse of 'Tractor' is oxymoronic, which really ought to mean stupid cow, but sadly doesn't. It's perhaps more accurate to describe it as paradoxical, which students of etymology will know ought to describe an emergency prostitute, but unfortunately doesn't. Instead, a paradox is the general term for anything that strikes us as credibly contradictory. An oxymoron is often described as a specific form of paradox. The images Hughes chooses about metal as the tractor succumbs to the vicious cold all combine to remind us of the dangerous business of making steel.

Later he calls it a metal trap he has walked into. All of this metallic ferocity takes place on a viciously cold winter's day. Yet it makes sense. We don't quibble or quarrel with him about the detail like some inept politician caught in the headlights of a radio interviewer, mumbling and fumbling over fantasy figures. We don't sit in front of the page shouting, 'But tractors don't have entrails, ice isn't molten and starlings can't blow smokily.' Quite the opposite: we delight in the realisation that this combination of words, in this shape and pattern, the sound and sense combined, let us into his experience in a way nothing else can. There is really only one response to great poetry: an unqualified, appreciative 'yes'.

Of course, not all poetry is great, and one of the ways you can tell is when you don't respond with that unqualified 'yes', when you find yourself struggling to understand the experience because the words, patterns and sounds the poet uses not only don't help you, they trip you up, get in your way like lazy tourists or just slap you in the face. Thomas Hardy puts it like this in his 1880 novel *The Trumpet-Major*:

> *But conversation, as such, was naturally at first of a nervous, tentative kind, in which, as in the works of some hazy poets, the sense was considerably led by the sound.* [1]

I defy anyone to deny their cheeks are smarting after reading Hardy's 'Dead "Wessex" the Dog to the Household'. Wessex was a fox terrier, and like lots of his kind, a bit of a thug. Stories of his misbehaviour lighten the pages of hefty biographies about Hardy, but however belligerent, cute or interesting this wiry little vulpephobe really was, Hardy's poem does absolutely nothing to help us discover.

> *Do you think of me at all,*
> *Wistful ones?*
> *Do you think of me at all*
> *As if nigh?*
> *Do you think of me at all*
> *At the creep of evenfall,*
> *Or when the sky-birds call*
> *As they fly?*

This is so saccharine and cloying, and sounds so predictable and clumsy that it drags you down long before you can get to the end. The only thing this particular dog lover thinks when he reads Hardy's poem is, 'I'm glad hairy-face is dead; at least that way we won't have to suffer any more verse like this.' Hardy wrote some beautiful poems but, clearly, even muses pull a sickie.

One of the aspects of poetry lots of metrophobes struggle

with is sound. Words describing sounds, like 'lyrical', 'melodic' or even the simplest of all, 'onomatopoeia' which is when a word like 'buzz' or 'quack' mimics the thing it describes, go straight in one ear and out the other, literally. Metrophobes don't hear them when they see them. 'Tractor' provides ideal medicine for this particular symptom. As Hughes sets to work to try and start this brute of a machine, which just seems to be getting colder and colder, he cranks it with an old-fashioned starting handle, which requires a lot of physical effort, and he even has the benefit of a modern aid and squirts one of those quick-start products into its carburettor, only to find it splutters. The tractor mocks his efforts and seems determined to stay where it is, frozen to the ground. But then comes a wonderful example of how to use sound and rhythm together to convey a sense of the experience to the person who wasn't there. Hughes describes that familiar sound of a motor repeatedly failing to start but does so in one sentence, deliberately and carefully punctuated so that we can almost hear that infuriating starter motor failing again and again to push the engine over the edge into firing properly. Until it does. Hughes forces you to read straight from one line and on into the next, technically called enjambment, and it works beautifully.

A glance at 'Tractor' on the page and you should notice a breaking down of the pattern and structure towards the end. The verses and lines become shorter. A couple of lines are only one word long and Hughes repeatedly opts for *and* as a rhythmical means to bring the whole thing to a dramatic, celebratory conclusion. What was a senseless heap of metal is transformed into a living, breathing creature bursting with life and vitality.

Anyone who has tried to start a recalcitrant vehicle, whatever the weather, will also appreciate how Hughes felt.

However scarring or futile your experience of poetry at school may have been, most people will remember something about simile and metaphor. The simile is an open acknowledgement of similarity between two things because it uses the words *as* or *like*, while the metaphor goes straight for the jugular, as it were (notice how I mixed the two there, just to make sure you're paying attention), and says one thing actually *is* another. Hughes comes up with a simile in 'Tractor' that is so imaginative and skilfully constructed as verse, it's well worth stopping to admire it. Once he has managed to fire the engine and the tractor has started to turn over, he produces a scintillating simile of it as some kind of diabolical being trying to materialise.

Now I've never seen a demon materialise, although I think I fell in love with one once, and I'm certainly not expert enough to know if one materialisation is more complete than another, yet I have not the least problem imagining this happening as I read it. How can that be? I'd argue it's because Hughes, like all writers, relies on his readers sharing something of his own history and culture. The ramifications of that, of course, are simply huge. We'll clamber onto them much later. Whether in art, in film or in literature, we kind of do know what a materialising devil looks like because we've read it or seen it before. So much successful verse is successful because it exploits our shared culture. Which is why the more you read, the more you enjoy reading. But his skill doesn't end there. Look at the alliterative 's' sound that starts in the first line but is picked up and carried into the second and then over into the third. Is the 'sh' of *Shuddering* that different aurally from the 'tion' of *materialisation*? Remember my advice to look carefully as well as listen? Hopefully by now you can hear the connection between *demon* and *demonstrating* as well as see it.

Before we leave 'Tractor' and Ted Hughes, it would be remiss of me not to say something about his life. I claimed at the end of the first essay that 'poets have always had something of a reputation for intensity and excess'. I used Sappho, Byron, Dylan Thomas and Sylvia Plath as examples. Sylvia Plath met Ted Hughes in Cambridge at a party in 1956. She quickly married him and their fraught and explosively creative relationship has been the focus of intense speculative debate, to the point of legal proceedings, ever since. During the seventies, that cauldron of bubbling feminism, that debate has involved the repeated desecration of Plath's gravestone when individuals took it upon themselves to deface it by chiselling Hughes's name off. Each time he put it back. Only two months before I was writing this, the *Guardian* newspaper had to amend an article it published claiming that letters from Sylvia Plath to her psychiatrist had been discovered that threw new light on what must be the most investigated literary marriage in history. That amendment by Hughes's widow Carol reads:

The claims allegedly made by Sylvia Plath in unpublished letters to her former psychiatrist, suggesting that she was beaten by her husband, Ted Hughes, days before she miscarried their second child are as absurd as they are shocking to anyone who knew Ted well.[2]

If you find you have an appetite for Hughes and Plath, there is a glut of material. Get stuck into it and you will quickly add to the nation's obesity problem. However controversial and disputed the critical and biographical claims made about these two important twentieth-century poets are, some stark, naked facts are worth swallowing.

Plath was a Fulbright Scholar with a well-documented history of mental illness and made a number of equally well-recorded attempts at suicide involving pills and a car. In 1963 she succeeded by putting her head in an oven. Her two children by Hughes were in the house with her, three-year-old Frieda and one-year-old Nicholas, but she blocked the kitchen off from the rest of the house with wet towels and they survived.

Hughes had an affair with a Jewish refugee, Assia Wevill. She had been pregnant by Hughes at the time Plath killed herself, but aborted the pregnancy. She lived with Hughes and the two surviving children, Frieda and Nicholas, in Devon after Plath's death, but they never married. Assia had a daughter, Alexandra Tatiana Elise, believed to have been fathered by Hughes, in 1965.

In 1969 Wevill too killed herself. She also sealed the kitchen door and window, but took Alexandra into the room with her, giving her sleeping pills before she turned the oven on. Alexandra was found dead lying beside her mother, aged four. In 2009 Nicholas hanged himself at his home in Alaska, aged forty-seven.

Ten

My Last Duchess
(1842)

Robert Browning (1812–1889)

An earlier, although far less frenetic poetic marriage than that between Hughes and Plath, took place in 1846 between Elizabeth Barrett and Robert Browning. In this case the more famous of the two poets was Elizabeth and, arguably, Robert's career only took off when he managed to lure Elizabeth away from her possessive father. They married in secret then lived together in Italy after Elizabeth's father disinherited her, although she wasn't singled out for special neglect; he refused to entertain marriage for all twelve of his children.

Elizabeth is one of the most enigmatic poets you are likely to encounter, partly because of the way she has been celebrated and promulgated on stage and in film, ever since she exchanged love letters with Robert. Even her pet spaniel, Flush, has been immortalised, courtesy of no less than Virginia Woolf, who wrote her 1933 biography of Elizabeth, *Flush: A Biography*, through the eyes of the poor creature's stream of consciousness. Naming a dog carries the same risk as christening a child, especially when you consider you are far more likely to have to shout its name out loud in a public space. Although to be fair to Elizabeth, in her day, long before Joseph Bazalgette built London's sewers, Flush was an entirely logical name for a gun dog.

Most of these portrayals of Elizabeth have her lolling about ineffectually in a state of poor but undiagnosed ill health on a chaise longue, while Robert kneels by her, wielding sonnets. You will find a particularly interesting photograph of her online with her young son, both sporting notably long, curly hair and looking remarkably like a pair of doting, well-trained spaniels sitting for a portrait. But the poem I want to introduce, or reintroduce you to, is not by Elizabeth but by her husband Robert. 'My Last Duchess' is, like other poems we've looked at, hugely popular with anthologists. Pull out any poetry anthology published after 1900 and there's a pretty safe bet Browning's ill-fated duchess is in there. We'll find out why as we discover more about it.

It's an example of a type of poem Browning is rightly famous for, the dramatic monologue. He's anything but an easy poet to get on with. He's still not really appreciated today as much as some of his less able contemporaries, arguably because he makes such huge demands on his reader. The dramatic monologue is by its very nature more demanding because it does everything at one remove. Instead of describing what it's like to start a tractor on a freezing cold winter's morning, as Hughes does, Browning would have invented a farmer or labourer to start the tractor for him and the interest and value of the poem would not be in the accuracy or vividness of the description, but in the undercurrents and characterisation. We'd be far more interested in why his farmer was out there and what he'd get up to when he got back home than in the natural world or how difficult it was to start the tractor.

Browning had an unusually bookish upbringing. He hated school and was educated mostly at home by tutors, with the aid of a private library of over 6,000 books his bibliophile father possessed. He learned Latin, Greek, French and Italian early in life, an advantage he shares with John Milton. He started to study Greek at university but, unlike Milton, wasn't a natural linguist and scholar, so he left to concentrate on writing poetry at home, where his family were wealthy enough to support him. Later in his life he referred to Italy as his 'university', and Italianate is an entirely useful way to think of his verse. 'My Last Duchess', set in the town of Ferrara, is a perfect example.

Ferrara, in the north-east of Italy between Bologna and Venice, is a typically spectacular Renaissance city. A love of beauty is as inbred in a place like Ferrara as a love of football is in Manchester, or banjo duets in an Alabama swamp. The modern world would do well to remember we owe a debt of immense gratitude to the greedy bankers who built it, and much of Italy, during the Renaissance. Their ghosts are probably patiently waiting to collect the interest. Browning was captivated by the beauty he found in Italy and it inspired much, if not all, of his verse. In 'My Last Duchess' he sets up a little dramatic scene for us to stand by and enjoy.

The BBC has even produced a short, dramatised film version online for school students. It's extraordinarily painful. An excruciatingly embarrassing example of what happens when people exchange their responsibility to educate for political correctness. It's a common characteristic of contemporary theatre, this desire to pervert the cultural origins of a play in order to satisfy the ephemeral politics of the day. It's one reason I don't go to the theatre anywhere near as often as I used to. I've no interest in seeing *Hamlet* staged in a Masai village, unless I'm actually in a Masai village, or *The Importance of Being Earnest* recreated in Mordor. I once made a special trip just to see *A Midsummer's Night's Dream* staged in a ruined French abbey on midsummer's eve. You don't make any work of art more accessible by cutting its cultural umbilical cord. You just cheapen it.

The scene Browning creates is between a wealthy Italian duke and a guest at his house, who is apparently there to negotiate a marriage dowry on behalf of his own, aristocratic employer, a mere count. It's generally accepted that the duke is based on a real life, historical figure, Duke Alfonso II, who ruled Ferrara between 1559 and 1597. The duchess is his first wife, Lucrezia de' Medici, who died in 1561 aged seventeen, possibly from tuberculosis. There was at the time nothing at all to suggest her husband had had her killed, and her father made sure his own doctor looked after her. But poisoning is almost synonymous with the Medicis and the passing of time has meant poor Lucrezia has succumbed to the family curse. Plenty of books for students today confidently assert that her husband poisoned her. I suspect most do so on the evidence of Browning's poem.

There is an especially striking portrait of her held in the permanent collection of the North Carolina Museum of Art, painted in 1560, when she would have been only sixteen, and attributed today to the artist Alessandro Allori and his assistants. For years people believed Bronzino painted it. Whoever wielded the brush and oils, she was undoubtedly a very beautiful girl and the artist had immense talent. But the question I find myself asking is not how did she die, but did Browning ever see this painting? Because if he did, I find the gulf between the naïve child described and so easily despatched in 'My Last Duchess', and the intelligent, sophisticated young woman Allori captured on panel fascinating, if not literally incredible. The painting may have been commissioned by her brother Francesco de' Medici, but all we can safely know is that it is first recorded in the collection of Viscount Wimborne, Sir Ivor Churchill Guest (1873–1939), and that it was sold at Christie's in London on 9 March 1923 as a Bronzino. There's no trace of it in Italy before Viscount Wimborne presumably acquired it on a Grand Tour.

The poem opens with the duke deliberately drawing his guest's attention to the portrait of his late wife. He keeps it behind a curtain and invites the guest to sit, the better to appreciate the artist's skill. Fra Pandolf, clearly a celebrated painter, is fictional, the Fra indicates he is a monk, and the duke's praise, *Looking as if she were alive. I call/That piece a wonder, now*, makes clear his painting is a true and impressive likeness. However, the dismissive way he chooses to describe the work it involved, *Fra Pandolf's hands/Worked busily a day*, exposes a hole in his aesthetics. It may indeed look like *there she stands*, but Fra Pandolf is after all just another rough-handed workman. This boasting about art as investment would be a *nouveau riche* cliché if the duke wasn't from one of the oldest families in

Italy, excessively proud of his *gift of a nine-hundred-years-old name*.

As the duke continues, it transpires that he grew jealous of his young wife's behaviour, of the way she spoke to Fra Pandolf and to others. The dramatic monologue form works subtly to kindle and inflame one of the most common forms of reading pleasure, irony. Irony is as common in literature as blank spaces between words. It is that sense we have of feeling privileged or clever, of knowing more than the characters do, of 'being in the know'. Irony is about seeing through things, and one of the most powerful social interactions human beings ever enjoy is exposing a lie. Without it there would be no international news industry. In the case of 'My Last Duchess', Browning doesn't just let his duke elegantly hang himself, he gets him to choose the rope, tie the knot neatly, then stick his own head in it. Word by word, his criticism of his late wife reveals aspects of his own character we deplore and fear. That unassuming little phrase, *if they durst*, carries an implicit threat, and exemplifies the way the duke operates. He is a lurid Machiavellian. However impressed or captivated the guest might be by the portrait, he says nothing. Unlike all the others who, seeing the portrait, have never failed to remark upon *The depth and passion of its earnest glance*, the duke claims, this *stranger* only *seemed* as if he would ask the same question. Ingeniously, Browning makes sure this guest remains tight-lipped. The duke poses the question on his behalf.

So rich is the irony in this poem that by the time we get to the end of it we empathise with a character who never even speaks. We're delighted he gets out of there without having to stutter,

'No thanks, I'm not thirsty,' as the duke offers him a frothing goblet of wine.

The *depth and passion* of that *earnest glance* provoke a whole raft of ideas. This is a really spectacular firework, especially if we think Browning's poem was indeed inspired by the Allori portrait now living in North Carolina. How far does the duke think his wife's behaviour fell short of what he expected? Does he want his guest to think she was flirtatious, naïve or openly unfaithful? *Depth* and *passion* are hardly the right words to describe a sixteen-year-old girl's day-to-day conversations with the adults around her. The duke's unfettered jealousy is evident in this observation:

> *Sir, 'twas not*
> *Her husband's presence only, called that spot*
> *Of joy into the Duchess' cheek;*

'Jealousy', like 'charisma' and 'icon', is a troubled word today. We often use it when what we really mean is envy. Jealousy really is that *green-eyed monster* Shakespeare evidently knew far too much about. It's an all-consuming passion that eats away at its victim every bit as inevitably and insidiously as terminal cancer. It brooks no reason, entertains no thought that isn't self-destructive and interprets the most innocent of actions as glaring infidelity. It is a sexual, not a moral disease. It's the price we all pay for love. Fortunately, few of us are forced to cash it in. However much the duke tries to dress his dissatisfaction up, we know he is jealous and that the expression Fra Pandolf captured is as faithful as it is pure. Which makes the duchess's fate, like Desdemona's, all the more pitiable and tragic. But the layers of irony are Black Forest gateau-thick. This Renaissance duke doesn't exist. Browning invented him and, as a Victorian middle-class male, what he invented is partly at least, Victorian, middle class and male.

Read the autobiography of Benvenuto Cellini, the Italian sculptor and goldsmith who was sixty-one when Lucrezia de' Medici died and you get a far better sense of what men in Ferrara must have been like. Cellini's book is an extraordinarily raw account of life in Renaissance Italy and does nothing to support Browning's Victorian imagination. Cellini even had connections with the d'Este family in Ferrara and created a portrait of the duke:

> *on a round piece of black stone, about the size of a little dinner plate. The Duke took great pleasure in my work, as well as in the many pleasant conversations we had together; and this meant that very often he would sit for his portrait for at least four or five hours, and several times he made me have supper with him.*[1]

Cellini stabbed and killed a rival in a street one night with impunity, and was himself poisoned with powdered glass on his lettuce, which only served to improve a long-standing digestive problem he suffered from. He also carried out numerous commissions for Lucrezia de' Medici's father, Cosimo I de' Medici.

Layers of irony this thick are another reason why it's vital not to cut the cultural umbilical cord of any work of art, but to trace it all the way back to its mother if you can.

So when we read 'My Last Duchess', the last thing we are treated to is a trip to the past, at least not to Renaissance Italy. Browning's poem says far more about the educated Victorian male's view of the world than a Machiavellian aristocrat's. And that realisation suddenly makes even more sense the moment you know that one of the important steps in Browning's career was when his early poem 'Pauline' was noticed by Christina Rossetti's artist brother Dante Gabriel, when presumably he was twiddling his oily thumbs one day in the Reading Room at the British Museum. Rossetti wrote to Browning in Italy and kick-started a correspondence that binds Browning to the Pre-Raphaelite Brotherhood as tightly as ivy round a naked nymph's ankle. Here are the first few lines of 'Pauline'.[2]

> *Pauline, mine own, bend o'er me – thy soft breast*
> *Shall pant to mine – bend o'er me – thy sweet eyes,*
> *And loosened hair, and breathing lips, arms*
> *Drawing me to thee – these build up a screen*
> *To shut me in with thee, and from all fear,*
> *So that I might unlock the sleepless brood*
> *Of fancies from my soul, their lurking place,*
> *Nor doubt that each would pass, ne'er to return*
> *To one so watched, so loved and so secured.*
> *But what can guard thee but thy naked love?*

You don't have to be an art historian to spot the hysterical connection between Browning's early poem and the gorgeous paintings reproduced on postcards in gallery gift shops from London to North Carolina. These chaps idealised and idolised the women they fell for. When you know that, the duke's warning to his guest appears far more Victorian than victorious. What breeds in Browning's poem is not the blue blood of a Renaissance prince but the red mist of a starched collar seduced by satin and silk.

The duke lists more transgressions by his young wife. She clearly appreciated the compliments Fra Pandolf paid her, the pleasure elicited from a sunset or from a bough of cherry blossom someone spontaneously offered her. Even the *white mule* she rode around the estate on, presumably another gift of her husband's, was a simple joy to her. Through the flawed lens of the duke's jealousy all these innocent courtesies become near-criminal acts. With a burgeoning sense of threat that takes his conversation completely away from the portrait, the duke explains how he reached the stage where he would no longer tolerate her behaviour and with chilling ambiguity he declares, *I gave commands;/Then all smiles stopped together.* Browning's control of rhythm here is masterly and the resounding silence that follows *together* is repeated in the subsequent line after *alive*.

'My Last Duchess' is in some ways a misnomer. The young Lucrezia de' Medici, however lovely in life or pristine in paint, is not the subject of the poem. Her husband is. In trying to intimidate or impress his guest, the duke makes a point that condemns him utterly in our eyes, but more interestingly I think, in Browning's. In the midst of an articulate, even eloquent account of his wife's failings, he denies he has any skill with words – *Even had you skill/In speech—which I have not* – before making a statement that screeches irony, like metal scraped across metal. Had he been able to speak to her, and had she been temperamentally inclined to listen, which he denies she ever was, he declares, *E'en then would be some stooping; and I choose/Never to stoop*.

Browning probably spent a good deal of time on his knees, literally as well as metaphorically, given Elizabeth Barrett's fondness for a chaise longue. Standing beneath a pedestal is a predisposition for any Pre-Raphaelite artist, so it's no surprise that Browning's duke refuses to bow the knee. It is in the end his misogyny that Browning loathes. Not just his inability to appreciate a beautiful work of art but to worship at its sacred source. Poor little Lucrezia, like so many other objects of artistic passion, is tragic not because she is secretly put to death by a jealous husband, but because she is unappreciated and unloved, except from afar, by the poet himself.

If Allori's painting is a skilful likeness of Browning's duchess, I suspect I know what the sixteen-year-old Lucrezia de' Medici might have had to say to the louche Robert Browning, himself captured in watercolour by Rossetti and hanging in the Fitzwilliam Museum in Cambridge today. And it wouldn't have been pretty.

My Last Duchess
Ferrara

That's my last Duchess painted on the wall,
Looking as if she were alive. I call
That piece a wonder, now; Fra Pandolf's hands
Worked busily a day, and there she stands.
Will't please you sit and look at her? I said
'Fra Pandolf' by design, for never read
Strangers like you that pictured countenance,
The depth and passion of its earnest glance,
But to myself they turned (since none puts by
The curtain I have drawn for you, but I)
And seemed as they would ask me, if they durst,
How such a glance came there; so, not the first
Are you to turn and ask thus. Sir, 'twas not
Her husband's presence only, called that spot
Of joy into the Duchess' cheek; perhaps
Fra Pandolf chanced to say, 'Her mantle laps
Over my lady's wrist too much,' or 'Paint
Must never hope to reproduce the faint
Half-flush that dies along her throat.' Such stuff
Was courtesy, she thought, and cause enough
For calling up that spot of joy. She had
A heart—how shall I say?—too soon made glad,
Too easily impressed; she liked whate'er
She looked on, and her looks went everywhere.
Sir, 'twas all one! My favour at her breast,

My Last Duchess

The dropping of the daylight in the West,
The bough of cherries some officious fool
Broke in the orchard for her, the white mule
She rode with round the terrace—all and each
Would draw from her alike the approving speech,
Or blush, at least. She thanked men—good! but thanked
Somehow—I know not how—as if she ranked
My gift of a nine-hundred-years-old name
With anybody's gift. Who'd stoop to blame
This sort of trifling? Even had you skill
In speech—which I have not—to make your will
Quite clear to such an one, and say, 'Just this
Or that in you disgusts me; here you miss,
Or there exceed the mark'—and if she let
Herself be lessoned so, nor plainly set
Her wits to yours, forsooth, and made excuse—
E'en then would be some stooping; and I choose
Never to stoop. Oh, sir, she smiled, no doubt,
Whene'er I passed her; but who passed without
Much the same smile? This grew; I gave commands;
Then all smiles stopped together. There she stands
As if alive. Will't please you rise? We'll meet
The company below, then. I repeat,
The Count your master's known munificence
Is ample warrant that no just pretense
Of mine for dowry will be disallowed;
Though his fair daughter's self, as I avowed
At starting, is my object. Nay, we'll go

Together down, sir. Notice Neptune, though,
Taming a sea-horse, thought a rarity,
Which Claus of Innsbruck cast in bronze for me!

Eleven

To His Coy Mistress
(1681)
Andrew Marvell (1621–1678)

Coy is a word we should use more often. Its etymology takes it back a long way to French and Latin words for quiet, but it has a wonderfully clipped, neat, matter-of-fact sound that somehow suits the concept. If you think of opposites, antonyms like brash or brazen, they sound as expansive as coy is terse. Today people often restrict its meaning and use it as a synonym for shy, but that isn't really the act it performs in the sexual circus. Historically coyness is a sham, a conscious ploy played by women who restrain only to entice. It is an oxymoron all by itself: one up on cherry tart. In Marvell's day a *mistress* might refer to any adult female – puritan or prostitute – but one who was coy knew what she was up to. Giving the poem this title suggests that whoever inspired it was already playing games. If you read or hear it as a conventionally one-sided seduction, as just eloquent rhetoric from a lovesick poet, which is how it is so often handled by teachers and critics, you will miss a lot to enjoy.

Marvell was that mythical of all hybrids, an MP as well as a poet. Enoch Powell was another. Marvell sat in the House of Commons for almost two decades between 1650 and 1678 and played an interesting role in the aftermath of the English Civil War. He tutored both the daughter of Thomas Fairfax, the most important Puritan military commander, and Oliver Cromwell's ward, William Dutton, which suggests the two most powerful and ruthless figures of the cursory English republic admired and respected him.[1] It's worth appreciating, following our look at Rosenberg and his contemporaries in chapter six, that this particular war was unusually costly in human life. Historians argue over the precise figures, as well as about how to estimate them, but they do agree it decimated the adult male population of these islands and killed a higher percentage of the population than the Great War. When you recall the sea of poppies at the Tower of London that citizens of these islands found so moving one hundred years after the Great War, the English Civil War stats are quite something to get your head round.

Marvell worked with John Milton in the Council of State, which was in effect the republic's executive body, running and managing all aspects of the new government after the war. Milton was not just a brilliant Latinist and linguist, making him invaluable in terms of international diplomacy; he was also an effective polemicist for the regicides. Unlike Charles I, and many of the regicides, Milton kept his head, but lost all influence after the Restoration of Charles II. Marvell did much better. He maintained his head *and* a healthy income as the MP for Hull. A lot of biographers credit Marvell with saving Milton's skin. Milton had been a loud and persuasive megaphone for the regicides, but there's not much evidence to go on apart from Marvell writing a glowing review to the second edition of *Paradise Lost*, published in 1674, in the form of a poem. However convoluted his politics, they throw precious little light on 'To His Coy Mistress', which takes place in a cerebral pastoral landscape devoid of the usual and convenient grassy knolls, flowery nooks and babbling brooks. Marvell's seduction is all in the mind.

Look at the poem on the page and, besides shorter than normal lines, one of the things that will strike you is the regular, rhyming couplets. Writing in this tightly controlled way risks sounding predictable, even childish, but Marvell resorts to enjambment, the carrying over of sense from one line to another unhindered by punctuation, frequently enough to make it possible for a skilful reader to sound almost as though there is no rhyme at all. If I pick out examples of enjambment instead of rhymes, you can see how this works. Below are the first eight lines of the poem with every use of enjambment picked out in bold type, which makes it easy to see how this effect counters the predictability of rhyme.

Had we but world enough and time,
This coyness, lady, were no crime.
We would sit down, and think which ***way***
To *walk, and pass our long love's day.*
Thou by the Indian Ganges' ***side***
Shouldst *rubies find; I by the tide*
Of Humber would complain. I ***would***
Love *you ten years before the flood,*

Marvell likes the mental discipline that rhyme enforces, but uses enjambment to counter its repetitive drawbacks.

Marvell's poem is definitely one for cake lovers. He wants it all. The opening lines make no attempt on anything but his mistress's mind. He calls her coyness a *crime* because they don't have the time to do all the luxurious, languid things he imagines them doing, and as the poem picks up speed he appeals directly to her intelligence, arguing logically throughout. Yet he can't resist the flattery ploy and lapses midway into the kind of fleshly hyperbole anyone who has read a lot of love poetry will recognise all too well.

> *An hundred years should go to praise*
> *Thine eyes, and on thy forehead gaze;*
> *Two hundred to adore each breast,*
> *But thirty thousand to the rest;*

'Oh, sir! I've never heard it called that before!' would be a perfectly sensible response. Cake gone. The whole poem treads a fine line between genuine wit and *Carry On up the Metaphysics*.

Exaggeration, usually called hyperbole in poetry, is a curiously discreet technique when you consider what it involves. Great poets have a remarkable ability to introduce astounding exaggeration into their verse without you even noticing. They toss the most outrageous claims into the flow of otherwise simple sentences, yet barely create a ripple.

I would
Love you ten years before the flood,
And you should, if you please, refuse
Till the conversion of the Jews.

This is fidelity on a geological timescale. This interest in exaggeration is far from limited to Marvell. Poets know it's a flexible tool and can make people laugh aloud just as effectively as it can move them to tears, or into bed. John Donne is a genius at it. Think of the most bizarre way to exaggerate something and he will take it to the next step, and make it sound entirely credible. In Marvell's poem it leads to one of the most well-known quotations in the entire history of English poetry.

But at my back I always hear
Time's wingèd chariot hurrying near;
And yonder all before us lie
Deserts of vast eternity.

That last line is a perfect example of the talent anyone needs to write poetry and not prose. That rapid-fire *But at my back*, with its crisp, short, stressed syllables is followed by a line almost as pacey, before the first syllable of *yonder* and the elongated sound of *all* slows everything to a walk, before a dead stop at *lie*. It's a fascinating example of the mechanics of poetry. There is no punctuation after *lie*, so the reader has to follow on, to *enjamb* as it were, onto the next line. But just try reading it aloud to make the enjambment sound obvious. The only way you can is to force a pause after *us* and if you do that, you undermine the sense of empty, extensive waste the natural stress on *Deserts* carries with it, which sounds so powerful together with the lengthy 'ah' sound of *vast*, and the way *eternity* falls away after the initial hard 'eh' sound.

Another way to appreciate this effect is just to look in isolation at that last line, *Deserts of vast eternity*, and experiment with reading it aloud. It's not easy, unless you trifle with it and go for *desserts*. Marvell's sense of sound, his ear for poetry, helps him see that those four words in that sequence convey exactly the sense of massive waste and boundlessness he wants his mistress to fear. Because if she fears it, she might just bite at the bait he immediately offers her.

Leaping ahead to both their deaths, he asks her to picture her own corpse, not something most young women do every day, I imagine. In a twist of wit worthy of Donne, he goes straight to the point and risks a really risqué argument, *then worms shall try/ That long-preserved virginity,* hardly a seductive image. He dismisses her *honour*, her determination to preserve her virginity, as *quaint*, which besides the obvious accusation of being inappropriate or precious, is an etymological minefield. The reasonable, logical, even sensitive respect for the girl's mind that began the poem turns into something more passionate, personal and sexual. She's either going to run a mile or his bluntness is going to expose her coyness. His passion he imagines wasted away as cruelly as her beauty, *And into ashes all my lust*, but in using that particular four-letter word, instead of 'love', he draws attention again to her coyness. To be bluntly prosaic: this is let's-not-beat-about-the-bush poetry.

He concludes this part of his argument with a chilling bit of logic driven forcefully home by the tight rhyme.

> *The grave's a fine and private place,*
> *But none, I think, do there embrace.*

What could any young girl say to that? He has driven her into a dark and lonely corner. If he had ended his poem there, it would be much the worse for it and, probably, him. But Marvell has more wit up his no doubt ornate and lacy sleeve. Turning his back on the dismal, funereal image he deliberately conjured up, he switches instantly and stresses the opposite, the *now*, a word he repeats three times in only six lines, twice at the very start of a line, where it carries maximum stress. His strategy is the conventional *carpe diem* familiar in lots of literature, in which writers urge us to make the most of life in the here and now, to relish and celebrate it. Regret is for wimps.

The final fourteen lines of the poem are dramatically different. Having hopefully assured her of the depth and fidelity of his lust for her and flattered her sufficiently in the first section, Marvell sets the clock ticking, then terrifies her with images of what they will both quickly become, dust and ashes. Finally, he offers her hope.

That hope starts by forgiving and forgetting her coyness. Instead he reflects back to her a sensual, vital and intense picture of herself at the height of her powers. There's some scholarship that argues the poem was written when Marvell was in his early thirties, and the age gap implied here certainly seems to support that.

> *while the youthful hue*
> *Sits on thy skin like morning dew,*
> *And while thy willing soul transpires*
> *At every pore with instant fires,*

There's admirable wit in that combination of the *morning dew* on her skin and the idea that her *willing soul* breathes through her pores not as moisture, but paradoxically as *instant fires*. She may wish to convey coyness, but he knows and she feels differently. Three hundred years later it's worth reminding ourselves that Marvell's admiration of her skin, that *youthful hue*, carried substantially more weight that it does today. His mistress lived in an age when the plague was a constant and very real fear, and a whole raft of unpleasant and often fatal diseases could destroy a girl's beauty, however renowned or admired, in days. Marvell was forty-four years old and an MP when the Great Plague swept through London, killing around a quarter of the population. Who knows, perhaps the girl this poem was designed to coax into bed was one of them? Even as late as Dickens, this kind of dramatic change in epidermal fortune wasn't unusual, as Esther Summerson discovers in his *Bleak House*. Smallpox ravishes her face to the point where one of her admirers, name of Guppy (to lapse into Dickensian for a moment), literally doesn't know where to look when he sees her new look. When you're bombarded with messages telling you you're worth it – whatever *it* is – as young girls today are, then perhaps Marvell's argument about her youth doesn't sound so persuasive.

Having put the weight of youth and vitality behind his argument, Marvell strides on with *carpe diem* in seven-league boots, imagining them enjoying each other in a series of images that are, remarkably ... coy, although admittedly the word *sport*, which he uses as a euphemism for sex in *Now let us sport us while we may*, has to be approached with some etymological caution. Its modern use around codified physical games or elite performance is quite recent and an extension of its original meaning, which is simply to amuse oneself or to take pleasure in some form of activity away from more serious matters. But when you think back to the overtly sexual way he addressed his mistress in their metaphorical tomb, it is striking that he reins in his language and imagery at the end of the poem and instead of the sensual, piquant sauce she's been invited to taste, she gets béchamel. First it's those *amorous birds of prey*, which is as close as we get to writhing, entwined limbs, and then it's that image of them as a strong and sweet *ball* tearing *Through the iron gates of life*, like some spectacularly New Model Army weapon designed to breach a siege.

The final couplet of the poem is a brave effort to redeem the situation:

> *Thus, though we cannot make our sun*
> *Stand still, yet we will make him run.*

A skilled reader can certainly convey the sense of fierce passion Marvell no doubt sought. But after the carefully constructed, skilful argument leading up to this call to *carpe diem* arms, there is something deflating about these last fourteen lines. I always feel a little cheated, short-changed, and can't help wondering if she felt that too. But that immediately makes me reflect on how determined by my own gender that response is, which sets a whole set of alarm bells ringing.

Current gender politics is so fluid, so fraught with pitfalls, that even if I were a participant, I can't imagine how I would keep up with the various factions. Some of the most famous names in admired, feminist literature have found themselves pilloried and harangued in recent months, so who am I to comment? But what I can comment on is how Marvell's poem compares to other love poetry.

Those last fourteen lines move away from the personal to the shared. They remind the reader just how precious a gift life – never mind love – is. Marvell's great achievement in this poem is not in the depth of passion he conveys, or the shallowness of his lust, but in the beautiful connection he draws between love and life, between sex and vitality. No one wants to look back at their life and see nothing but regret or missed opportunities. At a time in two people's lives when it's not too late, he seizes on that fear and turns it into *ashes* and *dust*. Perhaps that is why *Time's wingèd chariot* has become one of those rare quotations that has a life of its own, because in the end Marvell's 'To His Coy Mistress' is a love poem to life itself.

To His Coy Mistress

Had we but world enough and time,
This coyness, lady, were no crime.
We would sit down, and think which way
To walk, and pass our long love's day.
Thou by the Indian Ganges' side
Shouldst rubies find; I by the tide
Of Humber would complain. I would
Love you ten years before the flood,
And you should, if you please, refuse
Till the conversion of the Jews.
My vegetable love should grow
Vaster than empires and more slow;
An hundred years should go to praise
Thine eyes, and on thy forehead gaze;
Two hundred to adore each breast,
But thirty thousand to the rest;
An age at least to every part,
And the last age should show your heart.
For, lady, you deserve this state,
Nor would I love at lower rate.
   But at my back I always hear
Time's wingèd chariot hurrying near;
And yonder all before us lie
Deserts of vast eternity.
Thy beauty shall no more be found;
Nor, in thy marble vault, shall sound

My echoing song; then worms shall try
That long-preserved virginity,
And your quaint honour turn to dust,
And into ashes all my lust;
The grave's a fine and private place,
But none, I think, do there embrace.
   Now therefore, while the youthful hue
Sits on thy skin like morning dew,
And while thy willing soul transpires
At every pore with instant fires,
Now let us sport us while we may,
And now, like amorous birds of prey,
Rather at once our time devour
Than languish in his slow-chapped power.
Let us roll all our strength and all
Our sweetness up into one ball,
And tear our pleasures with rough strife
Through the iron gates of life:
Thus, though we cannot make our sun
Stand still, yet we will make him run.

Twelve

Famous for What?
(2014)
Hollie McNish (1983–)

Look up Hollie McNish and you will find her described not just as a YouTube sensation and British poet, but you will also discover she won the Ted Hughes Award for New Work in Poetry in 2017, an award that 'seeks to recognise excellence in poetry, highlighting outstanding contributions made by poets to our cultural life' and donated by Poet Laureate Carol Ann Duffy. McNish is living, breathing, passionate proof of why I wrote this book.

In an interview on the BBC Radio 4 programme *Today*,[1] McNish said after winning the award she had 'cried a lot'. I can understand why. She also said this:

> *Most people who come to my gigs – it's more through the themes rather than a love of poetry. It's more people who are interested in breastfeeding, or immigration, or whatever it is that I've been talking about, or adolescent sex so yeah, it's more kind of thematic.*

A Cambridge modern languages graduate, McNish embodies the reality that poetry has become so distant, so difficult and so poorly served by our education system that new audiences and new ways of reaching them, which don't rely on the printed book, have had to be found. McNish piggybacks the cultural appeal of a live music event to get what she writes to a large and admiring audience. Which goes part way to account for an interview in the *Huffington Post* with her that begins, 'When we think of poetry, we think of old men from hundreds of years ago, miserable and confused'.[2] I stress those are the interviewer's words, not hers. I, for one, would just like to excuse myself from that astoundingly presumptive little 'we', and suggest that the interviewer's choice of 'miserable' and 'confused' are equally speculative. I can just hear hordes of teachers' teeth gnashing at the thought that all their hard work results in such a tarnished view. Far from being current, there is something clichéd about this because it's only a short step from that misery and confusion to those hackneyed images of Wordsworth striding across the Lake District, communing with nature.

To counter this sort of impression, McNish has made skilful, professional use of YouTube to extend the range of her live performances. In her popular poem about breastfeeding, 'Embarrassed', McNish reads straight to camera, urging the words on, and relying on aural techniques to convey her passion and her ideas. The poem I've chosen is one commissioned by *The Economist* magazine, intended, curiously, for 9–12-year-olds, not major subscribers I imagine, which is called 'Famous for What?'[3]

In the borrowed voice, if not costume of a teacher, McNish describes a class full of adolescents, drowning in a sea of media sewage that equates success with money and fame with infamy. Researchers are only just beginning to appreciate just how dramatically mobile technologies, combined with social media apps, have affected teenagers especially. Such is the concern that, for the first time, we are hearing calls for legislation. When one girl in particular who *doesn't talk a lot you see just sits and licks her lip gloss in lessons* asserts confidently that she wants to be famous, McNish's teacher tries to make her and the entire class address that key question, *famous for what?* It's a theme that's concerned plenty of poets. Adrian Mitchell's poem 'Dumb Insolence' is a fairly recent example, D. H. Lawrence's 'Last Lesson of the Afternoon' is another.

To get the most metrophobic medicinal value out of this poem and to understand why McNish's success justifies this entire series of essays, you need to take a look at her poem on the printed page. Her work is part of a relatively new genre of English poetry that began in the sixties with poets like Mitchell and Roger McGough and has been developed since by others like Benjamin Zephaniah and John Cooper Clarke, which relies on live performance for its success. It is important to acknowledge this because it takes as its starting point the principle that poetry is meant to be listened to, it is an aural experience. However – and this is where McNish and performance poets like her face real challenges – take that live element away and look at what's written, and a whole raft of questions crop up that a live performance alone cannot answer.

What this chapter on McNish allows me to do is to highlight the dramatic difference between listening to a poem being performed and reading a poem silently, as we would any other form of writing. It's easy to appreciate the different experience of watching a performance of *Hamlet* in a large, formal theatre, surrounded by other people, all responding to the actors, the action and the verse, and sitting quietly in a library corner, reading a copy of the play to yourself. It's not so easy to apply the same aesthetic test to performance poetry. When we do, what emerges is fascinating, informative and culturally explosive. In early 2018 the poet Rebecca Watts, writing in the *PN Review*, published 'The Cult of the Noble Amateur', a detailed and highly critical account of McNish's work, which itself provoked outbursts of both antagonism and support. Here is a flavour.

> *Just as McNish insults those she expects to buy her books – condescending to an uneducated class with which she professes solidarity, while simultaneously rejecting her spoken-word roots – the critics and publishers who praise her for 'telling it like it is' debase us as readers by peddling writing of the poorest quality because they think this is all we deserve.*[4]

As with all the poems in this book, I'm eager to encourage you to discover in them what excites and interests you. So I've subjected McNish's poem to a test I hope does much more than allow you to take a partisan view about 'Famous for What?' Think of it as exercise, a necessary part of any metrophobe's cure.

That test has two distinct parts. The first is about performance.

Live poetry events are nothing new but have always been a minority sport. Even with someone like McNish, who has a considerable following, performance poetry still lies well outside the cultural lives of the majority of the population. There's something persistently paradoxical about these live events too. Almost always marketed as cutting edge and innovative, they are nothing of the sort. Darkened rooms at the top of narrow stairs at the end of even darker, city-centre alleys reflect the economics of live poetry, not its aesthetics. Aged seventeen, I had friends who would stand in front of a microphone and read their own poetry, in between live music pulverising you from speakers the size of wardrobes. As a student in London in the seventies I frequently enjoyed an entertaining night out above a pub or in a scruffy bookshop listening to poets being poets. I've seen some very famous names in some very unseemly settings. I touched on this aspect of poetry in chapter eight, where a supermarket, wine and cheese signified real class. The image performance poetry has of being louche and avant-garde is a sham. Cinema and fiction are full of parodies that exploit this connection between poetry and precocity in the public consciousness. However, because I haven't seen McNish perform live, what follows is based on her YouTube performances.

If you're unfamiliar with performance poetry then what may strike you initially about watching McNish perform 'Famous for What?' is the driving, forceful, high-speed manner in which the words are delivered. She speaks quickly, with relatively few pauses, and with positive intent. Viewers may find they struggle to keep up. This technique is common in performance poetry, and infuses the words with excitement through the way they are spoken. This leads to lengthy, difficult-to-discern sentences dictated, as Thomas Hardy would have spotted, more by rhythm and rhyme than sense. McNish emphasises words for their sound and their position in the overall soundscape as much as for their meaning. So she manages, impressively, to rhyme *Kim Kardashian* with *anything* effectively, not because the words in isolation are an especially tight rhyme, but because by reading the two lengthy sentences where they occur in a breathless, unpunctuated way, the rhyme is forced to the surface. Similarly she rhymes *taking* with *education* and *families* with *magazines*. There are more conventional rhyming couplets. *Floor* with *for* and *sight* with *limelight*, but her performance style coerces rhymes out of certain words that would not otherwise catch your ear. I think the surprise that creates is one of the reasons audiences respond so well to many performance poets; it's certainly a key reason audiences respond to rap lyrics.

However much I'd like to skirt around the word, punctuation is an issue that can't be ignored when thinking about performance poetry. Read the Economist Educational Foundation's printed version of 'Famous for What?' as you listen to McNish perform it, and you will notice distinct differences in the way the printed page is punctuated and the way she reads it. You will notice other differences, even whole words added in or taken out. That's not surprising for a performance poet who might want to improve and modify things, like any professional comedian does, depending on how an audience has reacted. I once saw a very famous stand-up comic perform live, using material from a recording I happened to have. It was identical in every minute detail. He repeated every pause, every ad lib and every self-deprecating little nuance *precisely* as he had performed it for the tape, and no doubt dozens of times before. Even the way he mocked late arrivals to the theatre was identical. His live performance appeared natural, relaxed and spontaneous. It was in reality rehearsed to death, probably a very slow and painful one.

If you take the Kardashian rhyme as an example, this is how it appeared in the print version. The poem was one of a number commissioned by the Economist Educational Foundation, the independent charity of the *Economist* newspaper. The Foundation runs the Burnet News Club, a programme for state schools that develops students' critical thinking and literacy skills through discussions about the news. The foundation was kind enough to provide me personally with a copy reproduced at the end of the chapter.

> *She said she wished she had shaped lips that kissed like Kim Kardashian*
> *I said me too they're really nice but that would not change anything*

The way McNish performs it is slightly different.[5] Like this.

> *She said she wished she had shaped lips that kissed like Kim Kardashian,*
> *I said me too they're really nice but that would not change anything.*

She pauses clearly after Kardashian (hence my comma) and even more strongly after anything (hence my full stop). What's far more interesting is that the rules of punctuation dictate that the lines should be written like this.

She said she wished she had shaped lips that kissed like Kim Kardashian,
I said, 'Me too, they're really nice, but that would not change anything.'

The difference is in reported and direct speech, which McNish mixes freely throughout the whole poem. *She said shut up, she's going to become famous and everybody laughed again* is another example where direct speech butts directly up against reported without any punctuation to indicate the change. Using the rules would break up the driving, insistent rhythm of McNish's performance. She reads the two Kardashian lines, each sixteen syllables long, as though they are rhythmically identical, whether or not they are. Performance poetry has minimal respect for the natural stress words carry with them, wherever they end up in a line. She sacrifices the value of using punctuation to determine sense in favour of rapid-fire fluency. That is why she is difficult to keep up with. How much of this is conscious and how much accidental we can have no way of knowing. Certainly if you follow the printed poem while listening to her perform it, she uses full stops and commas *in performance* much more than she does in print. I was able to count twelve lines that she clearly end-stops, but which in print have no punctuation signalling that to a reader.

McNish also uses a technique many performance poets use, deliberately inserting pauses directly to break up the very fluency that appears to be the guiding rule. These seem like pauses for breath, but if you read the poem yourself you discover they aren't. Here are two separate lines with these pauses indicated by a dash. Hopefully this won't be confused with the forward slash I've conventionally used previously to signal a break in a poetic line.

> *On – football fields or worldwide singing*
> *She doesn't talk a lot you see just sits and – licks her lip gloss*
>   *in lessons*

It's difficult to determine the reason behind these. Sometimes they seem to indicate a stress on the following word, sometimes not. They definitely capture one's attention.

In her interview with the *Huffington Post*, McNish has this to say about how her mother fuelled her interest in poetry.

> *I remember as a kid reading loads of poetry with her* – Please Mrs Butler – *a collection by Allan Ahlberg I read so much it almost fell apart. I love kids' poetry, funny rhymes. Then at school I got less and less interested in it. I'm not sure why. But I got really interested in song lyrics . . . I just loved wordy music. I was a real geek about stuff like that. But I never put it together with the poetry I was studying, which I never really liked.*[6]

That fascination with children's verse, with the humour in it, is evident in her own work.

> *I hear young people say this all the time they say it more and more*
> *She twitched a bit and bit her lip and looked down at the floor*

Writers never work in isolation. One of the few messages I've repeated in these essays is the way poetry is inevitably linked to the poetry that preceded it. How poets and artists influence each other provides rich pickings for the parodists in film and fiction mentioned earlier. Fans of writers as varied as Tony Hancock and Mel Brooks will know exactly what I mean. These essays have exposed some quite curious connections between real poets, but in this kind of wordplay it's easy to see McNish's love of children's writers. A writer like Allan Ahlberg is a direct descendant of writers like Hilaire Belloc and Spike Milligan. McNish joins in.

The second part of the test requires silently *reading* performance poetry and the results are undoubtedly perplexing. Look at 'Famous for What?' printed on a page and the extreme length of many of the lines is glaringly obvious. There are no verses; no easy-to-spot, visible rhymes jump off the page at you. The whole thing looks much like prose, like a newspaper cutting without the paragraphs. Throughout this book I have stressed that poetry is all about economy, that poets cram acres of meaning into square inches of words. McNish doesn't do that.

The dominant tone and style of all performance poetry is colloquial. Performance poets don't speak like BBC radio newsreaders. Formal, crystalline English is anathema to them. They thrive on what they think is the language of ordinary men, to use a phrase a previous generation of poets lived and died by. The argument goes something like this. If you want ordinary people to respond to your poetry, then use language ordinary people understand and recognise. But as we have seen again and again, what makes poetry special is precisely the part of it that takes language somewhere else, to new places the reader has never visited. And the reality is that what McNish and other performance poets write is only a semblance of ordinary speech. A good example occurs in these two lines:

Famous for inventing things you use or new discoveries
Famous for the places they have seen and been uncovering

That phrase, *been uncovering*, is completely credible as colloquial street talk, but look again at its forced link with *discoveries* and that internal rhyme, *seen and been* and it's as consciously constructed as lots of the poetry we have looked at so far. It really is *artful*. As linguists who study these things know, record ordinary speech and what you get is, frequently, incomplete, unstructured, rambling and even incomprehensible. Yet shared sense somehow fills the gaps between people. Poets can never hope to imitate this because their work is inherently one-sided. Harold Pinter's entire career demonstrates the truth of this. However much fans might respond to McNish's vocabulary, syntax and tone, it isn't 'real'. I think that's why I admire it: it's the brilliance of the deception.

I'm not surprised that, tested in this way, McNish's poetry becomes culturally explosive and provokes such a vehement reaction by other poets, like Rebecca Watts. McNish knows her fans aren't attracted to poetry *per se*; it's her topics that attract them. The more I thought about McNish's poetry, the more I started to entertain the idea that she herself was possibly metrophobic. She acknowledges that she completely missed out as a teenager and stepped deftly over poetry, going from nursery rhyme straight into song. That has not stopped her from gaining the most prestigious national award we currently offer poets.

I make no apology for including McNish in this book. Her success almost demands it. But I have tried to present her work to you in the same way I have dealt with her predecessors, pointing out things to admire and perhaps sometimes, things that may not work at all. I would be misleading you if I were to pretend that every poem you ever read and every poet whose work you decide to explore will delight and please you. I still choke on T. S. Eliot and I was once interviewed for his old job.

The art world has been riven with debate and dissension about what constitutes meaningful artistic effort ever since Magritte painted a picture of a pipe and denied it on the same canvas. The most prestigious Royal Academy Summer Exhibition prize in 2017 went to a video installation featuring boats carrying migrants across the Mediterranean. What I think we see in McNish – and she is not alone in this; there are a number of similar poets, like Rupi Kaur, whose work has been hugely popular on Instagram – is the same battle being fought out around poetry. Like it or not, it's a fight we all have a dog in.

Famous for What?

I asked my class what everyone wanted to be
And a lot of them told me a celebrity
In magazines in television
On football fields or worldwide singing
We went round the class with everyone giving an answer.
Then I asked her.
What do you want to be? What would be your dream job?
She said she was going to be famous, Miss
and everybody scoffed
She doesn't talk a lot you see just sits and licks her lip gloss
   in lessons
She said shut up, she's going become famous and every-
   body laughed again
I turned around and asked her 'for what then?
She looked shocked
And didn't understand
I said I'd like to hear your plans and how you'll get that life
   then
I repeated what I said I said
I said 'famous for what, then cos
I hear young people say this all the time they say it more
   and more
She twitched a bit and bit her lip and looked down at the
   floor
She said she just meant really famous, rich, and didn't really
   know what for

Famous for What?

Well bigger boobs and Big Brother that's all been done to death I said
A few have famous families who get them in ahead
Actors, sports and music stars they all work very hard I said
People who are famous are not all just the same
She said her best friend kissed a footballer now everybody knows her name
I said my best friend saved a life today and no one knows her face
Loads of folks are photographed for their clothes or who they kiss at night
But some are really famous for more than how they show their life
Famous TV chefs she says, I smile and say that's right
But there are famous people all around you might not know from sight
People who write your favourite stories but don't glory in the limelight
Many people who you'd think look boring I think you should look twice cos some are
Famous for inventing things you use or new discoveries
Famous for the places they have seen and been uncovering
Some are famous for the people or the countries that they help
Other folks are famous for the products that you buy they sell
Some people are famous for their songs or books or magazines

Not those in the photo spots but the ones who write behind the scenes
Some people are famous for drawing beautifully and adding things
She said she wished she had shaped lips that kissed like Kim Kardashian
I said me too they're really nice but that would not change anything
She said she cannot sing, I said to her so what
There are so many other things you could be famous for
She said she doesn't see those people
How would she ever choose
I said think about the things that really mean a lot to you
The things that make you happier the things you love to use
The rules you might not like or the laws that all affect you
She said she hates her school and the subjects that she's taking
I said then go become a famous Minister of Education
Cos someone is in charge of your school, your hospital, your food, your money
Someone decides on all the stuff you have to learn and study
What age you have to be to do things you want to do and play
People make up all the rules you have to follow every day
What medicines you use when ill or how much your work will pay

Famous for What?

Decide if you might go to war one day or how to lower violence rates
How many playgrounds we should build, how many plants or grass or trees
And none of these people are YouTube hit celebrities
But the affect they have upon your life is huge your friends your families
All I'm saying is not everyone that does stuff is in magazines
And there are so many options and you could do much more
And if you still want to be famous
Just remember to find out what for.

Thirteen

The Gun
(2006)
Vicki Feaver (1943–)

At one stage in my life, part of my job involved teaching teenagers to use a shotgun. The first thing I would do is hold up the gun for them to look at. Then I would ask them this question, 'This thing is a beautifully designed, effective tool. Like all tools it's designed to do a specific job really well. What job is it designed to do?' Their answers were often funny, never predictable and always wrong. I would inevitably have to spell out to them that it was a tool for killing living creatures – like them. When you first introduce anyone to a shotgun it's standard practice to load one barrel only because most have two. Those first, excitable pulls of the trigger can all too easily be followed by an involuntary second, straight into your face as they swing around seeking your approval. Guns may be fun but they're anything but funny. Innocent-looking names like Columbine, Breivik, Dunblane and now Stoneman Douglas hide catastrophic events it's difficult to contemplate with any clarity, their one common denominator being guns.

I ended the previous chapter on the sombre note that in the cultural battle taking place around poetry, we all have a dog in the fight. The reason I've chosen this poem, at this point in the book, is because so do our children.

To offer this poem successfully as another exercise in helping you become a keen devourer of poetry, I need to run a quick beginners' 101 about guns because it's a little word that hides a multitude of sins, committed most mortally by Hollywood, the video gaming industry and those who deny any connection between the fiction and the fact. I would also remind you that exercise can be stressful. This is definitely going to be the case with Vicki Feaver's 'The Gun'.

Guns come in a range of shapes, sizes and lethal potential, but in the UK, where their sale and use is sensibly controlled, there are two main types used for hunting. A rifle, which fires a single metal projectile called a bullet. And a shotgun, which fires a burst of small, round pieces of metal called shot out of a cartridge. Ideally you kill Bambi and other big stuff with a bullet from a rifle. You kill birds, Thumper and other furry, defenceless supper with shot from a shotgun.

In the UK at least, this seems a detail too far for many writers, TV directors and poets alike. No doubt in the USA, people queue up to thank the NRA for being better informed. I recently enjoyed an otherwise gorgeous TV adaptation of H. G. Wells's *The History of Mr Polly,* and if you know the novel you'll know Polly is only saved from being murdered when the gun used by local thug and drunk, Uncle Jim, blows up in his face. Tending to Polly after Jim has fled, in the presence of a policeman, TV

Nancy, Mr Polly's new love interest is relieved to see that the bullet's only grazed him, before the policeman adds that they have found the rifle. Which was a bit odd because the shotgun Jim actually carried and tried to murder Polly with was carefully shown in a cut-away with both its still smoking barrels split asunder. Watch that moment in the movie *Skyfall*, when the family retainer and elderly Scottish gamekeeper hands James Bond the only remaining firearm in the lonely house and be prepared never to enjoy any Bond film ever again. The gamekeeper reports grimly that all they have to protect themselves is his father's old hunting rifle as he places a beautiful, handcrafted, double-barrelled shotgun in Bond's hands. When a dour Scottish gamekeeper and 007 take hold of a shotgun but think it's a rifle, keep your eyes open for a tardy white rabbit and a little girl called Alice.

Some students seem to find 'The Gun' disturbing, even horrific. It doesn't make me laugh, certainly, but that's possibly because it speaks volumes it doesn't intend to. I chose it because it would be difficult to find a poem more timely in the wake of yet another mass school shooting in America. Vicki Feaver spent a long time living in Brixton, which is a London suburb with a chequered past, the kind of place that has moved from impoverished to gentrified without either the poor or the gentry having a say in it. Such areas often encapsulate what lazy journalists are trying to invoke when they use 'metropolitan liberal elite' as a kind of shorthand. So I wasn't surprised to find another poet, Matthew Sweeney, with the same background describe her work as 'domestic Gothic', which made me laugh aloud, but I don't think I was meant to.

The introduction to 'The Gun' on the Poetry Archive online says this.

> *I lived in Brixton in central London for twenty years and though I sometimes heard gunshots I never actually saw a gun. But now living in Lanarkshire, Scotland, right in the middle of the country I see lots of guns. Almost all the men seem to have a shotgun. And then my own husband got a shotgun and brought it into the house, and at first I felt very afraid of it and then gradually my whole attitude changed as I describe in this poem.*[1]

I lived and worked in central London for nine years, another four in north London and then another nineteen in south London. I never heard a gun in all that time and I'm even the proud owner of a commendation from the City of London Police for a preventing an armed robbery, under Blackfriars Bridge, which is about as central in London it's possible to get. The only guns I've ever seen in London have always been cradled tenderly like a babe in the arms of police officers who know exactly where the safety catch is and how to access it quickly, unlike the two French police officers I once saw strolling around Charles de Gaulle Airport dandling their assault rifles in one hand. I know which of the two I'd trust in an emergency, and this digression into the story the poet weaves behind the poem is, above all, a matter of trust.

Brixton is a part of south London that retains something of a poor but culturally 'cool' reputation, strangely as a result of rioting that took place there in 1981. That specific reference to hearing gunshots smacks all too loudly to me not of the genuine article, but of every middle-class Bohemian's urge to descend to street level in search of working-class credentials. It is the same urge we saw from Edith Nesbit in chapter four, stepping into a world of rural peasant traditions that attracted her to write 'The Things that Matter', but which she really knew little about. The condescension Rebecca Watts complained of, writing about Hollie McNish in the *PN Review*, involves the same kind of social class-skipping. Doubt any writer's honesty and their work quickly starts to unravel.

The entry on Vicki Feaver in the Poetry Archive online lists her favourite sayings about poetry. Amongst thoughtful words from writers as varied as Samuel Taylor Coleridge and Stevie Smith, they include this quotation from the radical American feminist, Adrienne Rich.

A poem is a construction of language that uses, tries to use everything that language can do to conjure [sic] *to summon up something thats* [sic] *not quite knowable in any other way.*

Hold that thought.

'The Gun' starts with an uncompromising statement that the rest of the poem bears out. Bring a gun into a house, into the sacred domestic setting of every family, regardless of its culture, religion, affluence or poverty, and you change things. A home with a gun in it is a different place. A study published in the journal of the American Academy of Pediatrics in June 2017 produced newspaper headlines claiming that nearly nineteen children a day in the USA die from or are treated for gunshot wounds. The study concluded that 1,300 children died as a result of a gun from 2012 to 2014 and nearly 6,000 were treated for gun-related injuries. Of those injured, 71 per cent were the result of assault while approximately 21 per cent were unintentional, often because children took their parents' guns without anyone's knowledge. Not difficult to imagine how some of those homes were changed. In the USA guns change schools too.

A Canadian journalist friend working in the Middle East once wrote an article about people buying guns and told me that while doing the research, he went into a store in Tel Aviv. When he asked the sweet-looking young girl behind the counter what kind of gun she might recommend, she replied, 'Well, personally I use this,' and, reaching into the waistline of her slim skirt behind her back, she pulled out her own, shiny, well-oiled killing tool.

The gun owner in the poem lays his shotgun down on the green-checked tablecloth in the kitchen, *stretched out like something dead/itself*, where it rests, *casting a grey shadow*. There is a fear of it from the start, which I imagine that morally upright tablecloth straight from the Bible Belt and no doubt fresh with flour from the apple pie cooking in the Aga, is meant to highlight. I can't help stifling a smile: more domestic goddess than domestic Gothic.

The third verse begins with *At first, it's just practice*, which is far too similar for comfort for me to Carol Ann Duffy's *At first, I visited, odd times,* from 'Mrs Midas' in chapter eight. Not simply because of the linguistic replication, but because both poems deal with wives and husbands, the way they communicate, or perhaps, more explicitly, the way these women think about their husbands. That unpretentious, barely noticeable little *At first* invites you to think 'what next?' There is a looming inevitability of implied criticism lurking behind it. It implies a change of heart.

The husband practises, *perforating tins* hanging from the branches of trees in the garden, *perforating* describing the few small holes any shotgun would make accurately and credibly. But then comes this blundering follow-up: *Then a rabbit shot/clean through the head.* For someone who later in the poem claims to enjoy joining in *the cooking: jointing/and slicing, stirring and tasting*, this is flagrantly and possibly fragrantly, erroneous, the same old bullet-hole fantasy that lazy writers fall for whenever shotguns are involved. *Clean through the head* might make Gotham City sense, but in the real world gunshot is so small it's not at all unusual only to discover it on the dinner plate or when it encounters your teeth. This is the kind of mistake that real yeoman poet Ted Hughes would have been horrified by, but not for 'Gothic' reasons. If you cast your mind back to the chapter on his poem 'Tractor', imagine it undermined by practical details that suggested he had never owned a tractor, never mind tried to start one on a freezing dawn in the Pennines. Feaver's carelessness has the same effect and it doesn't stop there.

The husband quickly progresses from practice in the garden to real-life killing. He is apparently such a good shot the fridge is quickly filled with free supper. His *hands reek of gun oil/and entrails*. This is presumably the kind of 'Gothic' description Matthew Sweeney admires, and indeed both guts and gun oil do smell differently from incense or cinnamon-spiced candles from M&S. In her desire to portray her man as an atavistic hunter-gatherer, she adds, *You trample/fur and feathers.* Now, the feathers I can see and understand. Anyone who has plucked anything will know how wistful, elusive and genuinely ticklish feathers are. They seem to gravitate towards your nose whatever precautions you take, but anyone who has skinned a rabbit or a hare will also know that you don't trample fur anywhere. Fur comes off with the skin, like a hairy onesie. It doesn't end up on the floor, unless you drop the whole thing.

This picture of her husband's transformation now culminates in the few lines I can't help feeling the entire poem was constructed around, like the first word placed in the middle of a Scrabble board. As though the entire poem was written outwards from this one idea.

> *There's a spring*
> *in your step; your eyes gleam*
> *like when sex was fresh.*

Remember Mrs Midas? She had similar issues with ageing.

> *You see, we were passionate then,*
> *in those halcyon days; unwrapping each other, rapidly,*
> *like presents, fast food.*

This is the kind of similarity that excites academics because they sniff a school of poetry in the making. I scent something else. I'm not suggesting anything as crude as imitation, which we all know is next to flattery. The echoes here are of something much more sophisticated and subtle. The distance, the dissatisfaction both these poetic heroines display hankers for contact outside the family they both purport to care for. One of the most discomfiting of all experiences you can have as a reader is that feeling you get when something strikes you as consciously crafted for a specific audience, from which you are definitely excluded. I don't believe it's a coincidence, for example, that *The Bookseller* informed its readers recently that one of the poems on an 'all-female shortlist' for a £10,000 poetry prize by the Irish literary magazine *The Moth*, was called 'A Gun in the House'.

I would be misleading you if I had only selected poems for this book that I loved or admired. Midway through, I chose deliberately to invite you to join me in thinking about several poems I find troubling, and in the case of 'The Gun', profoundly so because it purports to deal with such a sensitive, hugely significant issue.

On the face of it, 'The Gun' is a poem about transformational change and renewal. Sitting all alone and screaming significance is the single-line statement *A gun brings a house alive.* We are meant, of course, to be impressed by the cleverness of that paradox, to admire the way the poet has turned our expectations upside down; bringing death, dead things into the house now makes it seem more alive than ever. But when so much of what has preceded this claim appears fake, mere suburban guesswork, how can we respond with the applause and affirmation that is so obviously sought?

The final domestic image is of the wife preparing food and cooking with pleasure and happiness, *excited*, even if that excitement is tainted by the simile that concludes the poem.

> *as if the King of Death*
> *had arrived to feast, stalking*
> *out of winter woods,*
> *his black mouth*
> *sprouting golden crocuses.*

There's a barely disguised homage to Milton in the King of Death's black mouth. Milton does a stunning job of personifying massive abstract ideas like sin and death. In his epic *Paradise Lost*, the defining characteristic of Death, the monstrous progeny of Satan's incestuous rape of his own daughter Sin, is its insatiable appetite and vast, dark, cavernous maw. This King of Death is a more of a Muppet puppet, lumbering out of some TV-set dark forest with a fistful of flowers, ready for a song.

After many chapters devoted to admiring and enjoying poetry, this kind of criticism might come as something of a surprise. I make no apologies or excuses because I am on a mission to convince you that in poets you will find some of the most stimulating, exciting, provocative minds you are likely to encounter. That kind of undertaking is not without risk or disappointment. But as in the chapter on 'Mrs Midas', what matters is that you dig deeper than you might when sitting in the hairdresser's reading a magazine or flipping through a paperback on the commute every morning. Poetry is inherently provocative, an endless word game, with the added pleasure of sending you back into the real world with more in your head than when you left it for that brief period as you let the verse wash over or crash into you.

I agree with radical feminist Adrienne Rich, whom Vicki Feaver misquoted, when what she actually wrote was:

> *A poem is not a biographical anecdote. Finally a poem is a construction of language that uses, tries to use everything language can do, to conjure, to summon up something that's not quite knowable in any other way.*[2]

Words are not playthings, the Lego blocks of language. They are the currency of intelligence. Without them we convey and exchange little of significance. Abuse them, treat them carelessly, manipulate or contort them to suit your sense of self, or your clique's, and you commit an intellectual crime every bit as culturally damaging as the wild-eyed, unshaven maniac who takes a razor to a priceless canvas. A poem is not a biographical anecdote.

The Gun

Bringing a gun into a house
changes it.

You lay it on the kitchen table,
stretched out like something dead
itself: the grainy polished wood stock
jutting over the edge,
the long metal barrel
casting a grey shadow
on the green-checked cloth.

At first it's just practice:
perforating tins
dangling on orange string
from trees in the garden.
Then a rabbit shot
clean through the head.

Soon the fridge fills with creatures
that have run and flown.
Your hands reek of gun oil
and entrails. You trample
fur and feathers. There's a spring
in your step; your eyes gleam
like when sex was fresh.

A gun brings a house alive.

I join in the cooking: jointing
and slicing, stirring and tasting –
excited as if the King of Death
had arrived to feast, stalking
out of winter woods,
his black mouth
sprouting golden crocuses.

Fourteen

Twickenham Garden
(1633)
John Donne (1572–1631)

If ever you feel in need of a perfect poem, this is it: twenty-seven lines of staggeringly clever verse, as detailed and skilfully constructed as a Fabergé egg. A key reason I've chosen to write about it here was to provide the most striking possible contrast to the preceding poem, 'The Gun'. If that poem's use of pedestrian paradox impressed you, buckle up because Donne's wit is a bare-knuckle ride.

I stood in front of a portrait of John Donne in the National Portrait Gallery in London a few days ago. Most of the images we still have depict him with the neatly trimmed, pointy beard popular culture and commercial artists believe every Elizabethan or Jacobean gentleman sported. Guy Fawkes always has one. So tightly is this facial feature linked with Fawkes and anarchism, it's become a cheap badge of dishonour for anyone wanting to claim anti-state credentials. Guido Fawkes is of course one of the most successful libertarian political blogs, and the feature film *V for Vendetta* effectively commodified a symbolic representation of Fawkes's face built around that facial hair. It's now a rather sinister cheap, plastic mask available for anyone keen to brand himself a libertarian, without all the messy soul-searching.

One of the older schools in the UK is St Peter's School, York, a school that never celebrates 5 November. They think burning old boys is in bad taste. Fawkes, like Donne, was a Catholic in a Protestant nation but whereas Fawkes famously decided on direct action, Donne famously chose apostasy, and there are English Catholics today who haven't forgiven him. He eventually became the Dean of St Paul's and wrote some potent anti-Catholic texts.

But the portrait by an unknown artist I was looking at paints a different picture. Donne is young in it, about twenty-three years old, yet instead of the respectable beard, he has the soft, half-cocked, shadowy moustache of a teenager who hasn't yet bought his first razor. A black hat big enough for the Quangle Wangle and a fine lace collar combine to suggest he was fussy about his appearance. Recently restored, the picture is still strikingly dark, except for Donne's skin and that lace collar. His arms are folded and the one visible hand is slim and youthful. Those folded arms and the direction of his gaze imply defiance. An inscription in Latin above the voluminous hat adds to the effect and, like so much of his poetry, mingles sex with religion. Translated it reads, *O Lady, lighten our darkness*. Substitute *Lord* instead of *Lady* and you'd have a pretty straight quotation from Psalm 17. This portrait was painted many years before he eloped with seventeen-year-old Ann Moore, his employer's daughter, which led to days of imprisonment before their marriage and years of impoverishment after it. Like other poets featured in these essays, Donne's life was far from prosaic.

The Twickenham Garden in his poem and the grand house that went with it have vanished beneath less spectacular suburban lawns. It belonged to Lucy, Countess of Bedfordshire, who was a famous patron of the arts and of Donne in particular. A surviving plan of the garden shows it was a typically symmetrical, concentric combination of hedges and pathways, probably designed with order in mind rather than colour. Certainly not scent, unlike the French garden I once spent a wonderful afternoon in with my two little girls, which was dedicated entirely to smelly plants. Toddler heaven. Order becomes quite important when the world you inhabit is torn between rival religions.

Gardens of the period were peaceful, restorative, privileged and, of course, private places, and the character in Donne's poem is supposedly enjoying it, hoping to put a spring in his step since he is *Blasted with sighs, and surrounded by teares.* No beating around these bushes. He is in love and we know this by that ingenious connection between *sighs* and *teares*. One without the other could point to all kinds of psychological states but both? He has to be besotted. You may recall I warned you in chapter eleven that Donne takes hyperbole to whole different planet. 'Twickenham Garden' explodes with it in that first line. Donne can't just cry or weep like any normal disappointed lover. He has to really suffer.

It's impossible to know today how Donne's contemporaries reacted to his trick of mingling sex and religion. We're so used to the two being energetically coerced by all kinds of zealots, barbarians, fruitcakes and, frankly, the psychologically disturbed, a rational perspective is hard to find. Having written about Shakespeare, Donne and Milton in past works, I've spent more time than most paddling around in the muddy religious and secular waters of the period, so I'm prepared to hazard a view. If, for example, you consider the extremity and intensity of Catholic martyrs of the period, or the notion of Protestant despair, a bizarre but entirely rational condition that saw lots of otherwise intelligent Protestants hurling themselves off battlements or into cold, dark waters because John Calvin had convinced them there was absolutely nothing whatsoever they could do to save their souls, God had already rigged the election, then it's hard to avoid the conclusion that religion was, all joking aside, a deadly serious business. If so, Donne's wit must have been regarded as risqué, if not spiritually risky. I suspect he was a dangerous man to know. The Andy Warhol of his generation but with a depth of intellect Warhol abjured.

Religion permeates every thought, every image in the first verse of this poem. This little bit of Twickenham becomes *True Paradise*, the Garden of Eden, and love *the serpent*. Mixing his beastly metaphors a bit, he also refers to the mood he has brought with him into the garden as *The spider love,* which when you realise for Donne's readers inevitably meant a venomous insect, poor maligned, misunderstood arachnids though they were, makes clear sense and is less of a clash with serpents. Snakes remain indelibly poisonous creatures in the public imagination to this day. But the cherry on this particularly delicious slice of religious sex is his use of the spectacularly unwieldy *transubstantiates*. Almost as deft as fitting supercalifragilisticexpialidocious into a line without anyone noticing. If there is one concept, one word that sat at the heart of the Reformation, *transubstantiation* was it. One on side of the fence were those who still believed the bread and wine of the communion were in some mysteriously profound way transformed into the body and blood of Christ, while seeking greener grass were the Protestants. For their more ascetic minds, this ornate Catholic trait was just too weird. For the well educated, there was no sitting on this fence. Not unless you wanted to go straight to hell without passing Go.

Donne's intelligence is so powerful, so driven by argument that readers and even fans of his sometimes miss the delight of engaging with his wit. It's worth dwelling for a moment on the assumption he makes in the first verse that just because he is in love, all enjoyment of this otherwise beautiful garden, bursting with life in spring, is ruined. After all, his eyes and ears *Receive such balmes, as else cure everything;* the sights and sounds of this garden can apparently cure every other powerful emotion a young man is capable of feeling: frustration, anger, despair or even true grief, except love. If you can see the folly in that, then you are well on the way to orbiting planet hyperbole with Donne, because he knows that too, he's just waiting for you to catch up.

Wit is a word with a deep roots, and modern usage tends to plant it in shallow soil. The wit we are most often invited to relish appears on radio or TV panel shows, and although often genuinely amusing and entertaining, even quick, is something completely different from the intensely clever, reverberating games with language Donne plays. His verse issues constant invitations to keep up. So here's a little test for you, although I suppose it's as much a test of this entire book, since it relies on so many of the ideas and poems I've already encouraged you to enjoy. Verse two begins with these four lines.

> 'Twere wholesomer for me that winter did
> Benight the glory of this place,
> And that a grave frost did forbid
> These trees to laugh, and mocke mee to my face;

A *grave frost* and presumably everything else that accompanies a garden in winter would suit his mood better. Read those four lines again. Notice the precision of the alternate rhyme. Look and listen to those two simple words, *did forbid*. Notice that choice of *grave* to describe the frost. He didn't choose 'white' or 'cold', 'fierce' or 'silver'. He chose *grave*. Now notice that he chose *These* before *trees*. He didn't choose 'the' or 'those', 'such' or 'all', all of which we could readily substitute. He chose *These*. Now pause and ask yourself why.

If you can hear and see the internal rhymes between *did* and *forbid* and *These* and *trees*, if you spotted the connection between *glory* and *grave*, then you should be feeling pretty pleased with yourself. If you noticed the alliteration in *mock mee to my*, you should be feeling even prouder, and when you decide to read the whole poem, there is plenty more to admire in Donne's artful combinations of words. Now you're more than ready for the last bit of this little test.

We've repeatedly seen how poets manipulate words for effect. The word 'wholesome' isn't especially odd, even today, especially when used about food, although it would have been in common usage in Donne's deeply religious culture about other, less material things. To use it in its comparative form *is* unusual, which is grammatically what Donne does here by adding the 'er' ending, since it sounds clunky and the phrase 'more wholesome' would sound more natural and fluent. Why does he opt for that clumsier sounding *wholesomer* and what does the reader gain as a result?

If you've answered that question as I hope you have, your relationship with the narrator of 'Twickenham Garden' will have shifted slightly. Irony, that rich spring of meaning that bubbles up through the gap between what is written and what is meant, will have caused you to think more deeply about this young man, his intentions and his sincerity. It will have nudged you to think about the recipient of this poem, the unknown, invisible source of all this excess. I know I'm a prisoner of gender, but when Donne does this, my reaction usually is – to abuse a contemporary phrase that is just itching to be abused – she must be worth it. If a love poem doesn't flatter, is it even a love poem?

If you have heard the phrase 'metaphysical poetry' before it won't be from me. I've avoided the term until now, even though Donne is the most famous of the metaphysical poets, who, by the way, include Andrew Marvell. It's perfectly sensible and useful for a formal student of literature to care about these kinds of labels, but as I've stressed throughout, this book isn't for them. But I do think as far as 'Twickenham Garden' goes, it's worth pointing out that when Samuel Johnson first coined the term 'metaphysical poet' what he was essentially doing was trying to connect a small number of poets writing in a short period of English history, not so much by what they wrote about, but by their distinctive and unusual style. And there is one aspect of that style that it's well worth not just coming to terms with, but handing over to one's solicitor before getting them to draft a binding contract signed and witnessed in front of a neutral third party. In poetry it's called a conceit.

A conceit is a metaphor that is somehow surprising, often delightfully so, and which appeals as much to our sense of the poet's intellectual ability as it does to anything else. In even simpler terms, conceits make us think the poet's really clever, and they know it.

They can be drawn out at some length, sometimes throughout an entire poem, and form a kind of intellectual framework for the rest of the poem to either be admired or to hang itself on. The one everyone uses as the model comes from Donne's poem 'A Valediction Forbidding Mourning', in which he imagines he and the woman he loves are like the feet of a compass. She is the fixed, firm foot pinned in the centre, while demands on him means he has to travel away from her, yet however far or whatever direction he moves, he is part of her and will always return to her, just like that second leg of the compass. Not obviously flattering, but that is the point.

At the end of the second verse of 'Twickenham Garden' Donne produces two absolute gems. Since he's miserably in love, he suggests he'd be better off if he became some inanimate feature of the garden, *Some senselesse piece of this place be*, so that he wouldn't have to feel all that pain. I guess she hasn't slept with him yet. The first suggestion is that he should be turned into a *mandrake*, which is a plant Donne's readers would have associated with all kinds of superstitious ideas completely lost to us today, the key one being the forked root's similarity to human form and uncanny ability to groan when pulled out of the ground. It's the second conceit he prefers. This time he suggests Love turn him into *a stone fountaine weeping out my yeare*. The weeping is obvious and for Donne, merely the springboard for far more impressive intellectual acrobatics. In the first part of the final verse he ties sex and religion together in an intricate knot woven out of individual images and words he has carefully chosen from the start to do exactly that.

> *Hither with christall vyals, lovers come,*
> *And take my teares, which are loves wine,*
> *And try your mistresse Teares at home,*
> *For all are false, that tast not just like mine;*

Visitors to Donne's lachrymose, hyperbolic fountain don't bring cups, jugs or bottles. They bring *christall vyals* to catch his overflowing tears and like ardent pilgrims they drink *loves wine* as a kind of test of faith, because if their mistresses' tears don't taste exactly like his, then those mistresses *all are false*. The intricate knot that began when he took hold of that unwieldy, impossibly awkward word *transubstantiates* in one hand, while keeping the other behind his back, begins to tighten in front of our disbelieving eyes. There is something magical, something deliberately deceptive, about the way Donne writes. He sends your mind one way so that in the end, when all is revealed, you stand amazed, asking yourself, 'How can anyone do that?'

This is so much more than merely secular wit. There is real danger in poetry like this at a time when foreign nations trained Jesuit priests then shipped them secretly back to England to reinstate the true faith, and foreign rulers believed it was their God-given duty to reverse the Reformation Henry VIII's lust had initiated in England. In 1593 Donne's own brother Henry died in Newgate Prison from plague, after having been arrested for harbouring a Jesuit. Henry betrayed the priest when threatened with torture. Playing with sex and religion in this way was not for the faint-hearted.

If the fountain conceit wasn't enough, he follows it with two brilliantly accusatory images aimed at provoking guilt and perhaps even a change of heart in that invisible goddess.

> *Alas, hearts do not in eyes shine,*
> *Nor can you more judge womans thoughts by teares,*
> *Than by her shadow what she weares.*

There is something utterly beautiful and terribly sad about the idiomatic expression Donne invokes for his comparison between a woman's thoughts and her clothes. It sounds undeniable, as though it's something we all know for sure. It leads naturally to a closing couplet that no one but Donne could have written.

Like a cross between a cryptic-crossword clue and an epitaph to someone you loved.

> *O perverse sexe, where none is true but shee,*
> *Who's therefore true, because her truth kills mee.*

Were this a book for students, I would have been happy to dive straight in and explore the various ways others have responded to these lines, as well as to offer some thoughts of my own. But it would be taking that bright, fizzing sparkler out of your hand just at the point when the firework has been set up ready for you to light. Instead I'll invite you to enjoy the display and then to reflect on what another famous poet wrote about Donne.

Coleridge was a huge fan of Donne's. He wrote:

If you would teach a scholar in the highest form how to read, take Donne ... When he has learned to read Donne, with all the force and meaning which are involved in the words, then send him to Milton and he will stalk on like a master, enjoying his walk.[1]

One reason, amongst many, that I've saved Milton for later. Enjoy the fireworks in Twickenham's lovely, timeless garden.

Twickenham Garden

Blasted with sighs, and surrounded with teares,
Hither I come to seeke the spring,
But at mine eyes, and at mine ears,
Receive such balmes, as else cure every thing;
But O, selfe traytor, I do bring
The spider love, which transubstantiates all,
And can convert Manna to gall,
And that this place may thoroughly be thought
True Paradise, I have the serpent brought.

'Twere wholesomer for mee, that winter did
Benight the glory of this place,
And that a grave frost did forbid
These trees to laugh, and mocke mee to my face;
But that I may not this disgrace
Indure, nor yet leave loving. Love, let mee
Some senselesse piece of this place bee;
Make me a mandrake, so I may groan here,
Or a stone fountaine weeping out my yeare.

Hither with christall vyals, lovers come,
And take my teares, which are loves wine,
And try your mistresse Teares at home,
For all are false, that tast not just like mine;
Alas, hearts do not in eyes shine,
Nor can you more judge womans thoughts by teares,

Twickenham Garden

Than by her shadow what she weares.
O perverse sexe, where none is true but shee,
Who's therefore true, because her truth kills mee.

Fifteen

Blackberry-Picking
(1966)
Seamus Heaney (1939–2013)

Seamus Heaney died in 2013 after a life wholly devoted to poetry. He held key roles at both Oxford and Harvard universities dedicated to poetry and won the Nobel Prize for Literature 'for works of lyrical beauty and ethical depth, which exalt everyday miracles and the living past', presumably not by the same judging panel that awarded the prize to Bob Dylan in 2016 'for having created new poetic expressions within the great American song tradition'.

Speaking to journalists after that 2016 announcement, Sara Danius, permanent secretary of the Swedish Academy, compared Dylan specifically to Sappho and Homer (the classical Greek poet, not Simpson, in case you're not sure) because they all used music, adding, 'He is a great poet in the grand English poetic tradition.' Bob Dylan is many impressive and laudable things, but if he's 'a great poet in the grand English tradition' then an outside bet on Donald Trump winning the prize in future for his tweets is definitely worth a punt.

Heaney was, like Donne, a Catholic brought up in a Protestant nation, in his case Northern Ireland and during a period we have come to call, with typically Irish understatement, the Troubles. A sustained period of internecine civil strife in the USA would probably have been called the Chaos or in France, *les Meurtres*. Unlike so many of his contemporaries, Heaney somehow managed to write about this period, even its politics, without ever being defined or confined by it. As an Englishman with an Irish Catholic mother and an English Catholic father, I grew up observing the Troubles with a degree of personal interest and a lot of confusion. As a student in London and later working in the City, apart from being constantly frustrated by the lack of litter bins, I found myself in deserted London streets on several occasions as scores of vehicles with blue flashing lights raced by. My place of work was only a five-minute walk away from the Baltic Exchange and Bishopsgate when both sites were devastated by huge car bombs placed by the IRA in 1992 and 1993. The Baltic Exchange bomb exploded on a Friday evening at 9.20 p.m., when the City was full of people socialising after work. It killed three people and injured ninety-one. The Bishopsgate bomb mercifully exploded on a Saturday morning when, as anyone who has worked in the City knows, the entire Square Mile is like a morgue anyway. One man died and forty-four people were injured, although the aftermath was appalling to see and it caused £350 million damage.

In all that period only one voice still resonates with me. BBC Radio interviewed a Belfast surgeon who had spent much of his career reconstructing the shattered parts of people caught up in the Troubles. Stressing how local, how absurdly few in number were the streets the source of all this misery and destruction came from, he said, 'You have to appreciate, these are small men with small arguments.' In July 2017, like millions of other television viewers, I watched one of these men, now in his seventies, attempting to apologise to victims of bombs he had assembled with his own hands, which killed twenty-one people and injured 182 in Birmingham pubs in 1974.

We will always need poets because they are the only men and women who insist there's a difference between apology and justice.

The poem I've chosen by Heaney, 'Blackberry-Picking', isn't one with any political overtones or overt connections but it's entirely typical of the work that brought him success. I've chosen it more because it comes from a collection called *Death of a Naturalist*. In an era where most people's connection with the natural world is filtered through the anthropomorphic lenses of BBC wildlife cameras, Heaney's poems about the natural world have far more to offer. In it he goes back to his childhood and the intense memory of picking blackberries in the fields around the village in County Derry where he grew up.

If you look at the poem on the page, you can see it is written in rhyming couplets but that the rhymes are especially varied. Heaney rhymes *clot* easily with *knot* but he also rhymes *sweet* with *it* and *peppered* with *Bluebeard's*. He has an ear for rhyme that often surprises. The poem begins with as inventive a rhyme as you are likely to find anywhere.

Blackberry-Picking

> *Late August, given heavy rain and sun*
> *For a full week, the blackberries would ripen.*

In 'Mr Tambourine Man' Dylan resorts to *run* to accompany *sun*, but he does raise his game and rhyme *realize* with *alibis* and *diplomat* with *cat* in 'Like a Rolling Stone'.

Heaney then describes evocatively how he and his childhood companions would go out armed with all kinds of impromptu vessels to collect blackberries from the local hedgerows. Some impressively fine detail helps him relive that childhood memory. Some of the berries they pick are a *glossy purple clot*, while others are *green, hard as a knot*. The *wet grass bleached our boots* and the children's *hands were peppered/With thorn pricks*, a sensation anyone who has picked blackberries will instantly recognise. These are admirably well-observed, sensual details that appeal as much to a taste for nostalgia as free fruit. Heaney has a real gift for descriptive power. He frequently finds a combination of words so perfect you're forced, like Rosenberg's cosmopolitan rat, *to inwardly grin* at his ingenuity. Tasting that first blackberry was *Like thickened wine*, and as the days progressed he describes the way the berries ripened with the kind of skill that most poets would die for, *Then red ones inked up*. If you can find a more perfect way to describe that process, I think I have a career suggestion for you. His finely tuned ear is evident too in the lists he uses: *milk cans, pea tins, jam-pots* and *hayfields, cornfields and potato-drills*. However mundane they are as isolated words, they become captivating together. Bob Dylan is a musician whose performances include words. Heaney was a poet who understood the music within words.

But the pleasure in gathering and hoarding the fruit ends in disappointment as the bathtub they filled with fruit quickly succumbed to the inevitable signs of decay *A rat-grey fungus, glutting on our cache*. The poem ends with a far-reaching lesson.

> *It wasn't fair*
> *That all the lovely canfuls smelt of rot.*
> *Each year I hoped they'd keep, knew they would not.*

There are other moments in his collection *Death of a Naturalist* when children learn hard truths. In a poem called 'The Early Purges', the young Heaney watches a local farmer drown a litter of kittens in a bucket as *Like wet gloves they bobbed and shone till he sluiced/Them out on the dunghill, glossy and dead*. Heaney's naturalist is one Ted Hughes would have admired, someone with little room for anthropomorphism and none at all for unicorns. For both these poets nature, however beautiful or inspirational, is implacable. An essential part of growing up is acknowledging that.

In chapter two, writing about George Mackay Brown, I made the point that only recently mankind turned a monumental historic corner because for the first time in human evolution, most of us now live in cities. The opportunity children have had for millennia to grow up and learn how uniquely dependent on the natural world we are as living beings, to appreciate where food comes from, how the weather impacts on our lives and the physical limitations of the shape we all inhabit has all but gone.

Like Heaney I was lucky enough to enjoy a childhood spent mostly under beautiful skies breathing clean air. It even included some holidays spent with family in the remote west of Ireland, digging and stacking peat in an Irish bog, churning butter and stacking hay. These richly redolent experiences stay rooted in my head because of the intense, unique smells that went with them. Although I'm sure a neuroscientist would think that mundane, I find it amazing.

For almost a decade I lived on the tenth floor of a block of flats in genuinely central London, and it was not unusual for me to have to go back up in the lift to get a coat because until you stepped out of the ground-floor entrance, you had no idea what the weather was really like. I hated that feeling of being disconnected from the natural world.

Walks were the staple diet of play as a young child. They would last all day, go on for miles and involve all kinds of unpredictable adventures involving trees, streams, wild birds and farm animals. On one occasion one of my elder brothers crawled over a fallen tree that had conveniently formed a bridge over a broad stream we often explored. Looking down into the water, he suddenly reached beneath the tree and started scrabbling around in the gravel on the bed of the stream. Triumphantly he raised a dripping hand in which he clutched half a dozen shiny brass objects. Even I realised straight away that those shining, pointed, slim things he was cradling in the palm of his hand were bullets.

This was shortly after the Second World War and the countryside had been one huge training ground for the military. On another occasion we found a rusting Tommy's helmet in a ditch. Back home and in secret, my brother prised what we now knew were 303 machine-gun bullet cases open and tipped the explosive, which looked like tiny, round elastic bands, into a little heap onto the fireplace. They flared up spectacularly and satisfyingly when he put a match to them.

A little older and a lot more independent, and my lengthy walks became all about catching fish or hunting with dogs. My friend and I once carried one of his dogs many miles home in a stretcher we made by shoving two young saplings down the sleeves of his coat, after it had broken its neck hitting a tree at full speed as it bent to pick up a rabbit. One day was spent repeatedly collapsing into uncontrollable fits laughter after one of the dogs that always accompanied us had cocked its leg and urinated on an electric fence. Pavements don't issue the same invitation to a child. They cut them off from the earth and dictate the direction they must go.

One word stands out for me at the end of Heaney's poem because it features so prominently in contemporary political discourse. If you are a responsible citizen who watches television news or current affairs programming, and listens to serious radio in order to feel informed, you will hear it constantly. Knowing as he did that hoarding the fruit would only *turn sour*, Heaney's childish self resorts to childish language to describe his emotion: *It wasn't fair*, he complains. Fairness is a concept born in the playground. Justice is for grown-ups. Yet again and again you will hear professional politicians use the term to cast a spotlight on something they perceive as a wrong that needs righting. They have the wrong homonym. It's not righting but writing they need.

The lesson 'Blackberry-Picking' and *Death of a Naturalist* teach is that nothing in the natural world we inhabit is fair. It is indicative of the quality of our political class, the poverty of their education, the suburbanity of their lived experience and inability to represent people outside their own snug and smug milieu that they insist on using it so freely and confidently, when the English language offers far more useful, eloquent options.

Blackberry-Picking

Late August, given heavy rain and sun
For a full week, the blackberries would ripen.
At first, just one, a glossy purple clot
Among others, red, green, hard as a knot.
You ate that first one and its flesh was sweet
Like thickened wine: summer's blood was in it
Leaving stains upon the tongue and lust for
Picking. Then red ones inked up and that hunger
Sent us out with milk cans, pea tins, jam-pots
Where briars scratched and wet grass bleached our boots.
Round hayfields, cornfields and potato-drills
We trekked and picked until the cans were full,
Until the tinkling bottom had been covered
With green ones, and on top big dark blobs burned
Like a plate of eyes. Our hands were peppered
With thorn pricks, our palms sticky as Bluebeard's.

We hoarded the fresh berries in the byre.
But when the bath was filled we found a fur,
A rat-grey fungus, glutting on our cache.
The juice was stinking too. Once off the bush
The fruit fermented, the sweet flesh would turn sour.
I always felt like crying. It wasn't fair
That all the lovely canfuls smelt of rot.
Each year I hoped they'd keep, knew they would not.

Sixteen

The Darkling Thrush
(1900)
Thomas Hardy (1840–1928)

Look *darkling* up in a decent dictionary and you will find it comes with the tag 'literary', indicating its use tends to be restricted to poets. What a shame such a useful adjective, one so easy to understand, so organically tied to the experience it describes isn't used more widely. 'Twilight' is pleasing enough and has a logic most users wouldn't stop to question but *darkling* is in a different league of sentiment. It harks back to the previous essay's reflections on our relationship with the natural world. When your daily experience of that unpredictable few minutes of every twenty-four hours when day gives way to night is poisoned by the fact that you can't even see the sky, or by the sulphurous glare of street lamps, lurid car headlights and blaring shop windows, maybe there's simply no use for a word like *darkling*.

One winter's night I was driving home along Streatham High Street, the kind of wide, bustling, multicultural street that threads through the heart of suburbs and sub-sections of cities all over the UK. There was a local power failure and the only light came from vehicles on the streets. The darkness and, strangely, the silence above and on either side of the car was intense, solid. Then a glow appeared high above me in a building, the light from a candle someone had managed to find and light, presumably in their flat, then another and another. As I drove slowly along, the two high walls of blackness on either side of the road became spattered with small, warm, dancing windows of light and suddenly the people behind those walls seemed more real, more alive. I wonder how long this obsession with metropolitan living will really last.

Most people will know Thomas Hardy from his great novels and some will know that he was a prolific poet too. They might not know that Hardy took such exception to the way his novel *Tess of the D'Urbervilles* was decried in public, that in effect he turned his back on fiction in favour of poetry and preferred to think of himself as a poet, not a novelist. He published over a thousand poems during his lifetime. Hardy is almost a parody poet. His ashes were placed in Poet's Corner in Westminster Abbey, but his heart was buried in the churchyard of St Michael's Church, Stinsford, in Dorset, beside graves occupied by his two wives. When his first wife Emma died in 1912, he wrote a series of poems about his relationship with her that are some of the most poignant, intimately personal and unusually honest poems you will ever read. Hopefully your meeting with his 'Darkling Thrush' will tempt you to read more and especially what critics today call his 'great poems' of 1912 to 1913, or just the '12 to 13 poems'.

'The Darkling Thrush' is one of his lyrical poems. Although everyone seems to agree it was first printed in *The Graphic* magazine on 29 December 1900, there's some confusion amongst Hardy fans about whether it was originally called 'The Century's End, 1900' or 'By the Century's Deathbed'. Speaking of which, I still shudder at the memory of witnessing Tony and Cherie Blair singing 'Auld Lang Syne' next to Queen Elizabeth II in that mercifully forgotten monument to Nu Labour's monumental ego and profligacy, the Dome, on a similar day a hundred years later. Hardy describes being alone, leaning on a frosty farm gate at the end of a bitterly cold winter's day, when a thrush starts to sing. It's difficult to imagine two more dramatically contrasting ways to celebrate the passing of a century, or two more revealing illustrations of differing human values.

Great poems are often built on the slightest foundations. There's a parallel to be drawn between that and Hardy's ability to find significance in such an apparently slight event, a thrush singing at twilight. He isn't the only one, of course. Many poets share this rare capacity to find extraordinary thoughts in ordinary events. Like Michelangelo with his block of marble, what Hardy finds is equally miraculous.

Before we get to that, I want to take the opportunity 'The Darkling Thrush' provides, especially after the last chapter's Nobel distractions, to consider what makes a poem lyrical. The word has ancient Greek origins connected to a harp-like musical instrument we never hear or see any more, except in fanciful images, the lyre. A lyric is, narrowly speaking, a series of words to be sung with a musical accompaniment, whether by Maria Callas or Leonard Cohen. But a lyric poem is more than that. It's usually a short poem, although short is a decidedly elastic term, with a single speaker or voice, who expresses personal, powerful feelings or perceptions reflectively or meditatively. Run another little test and think back to previous chapters and poems, then ask yourself which now strike you most strongly as lyrical poems? I hope 'The Tyger', 'Adlestrop' and 'When I am dead, my dearest' come straight to mind, as will 'The Gun', 'Tractor', 'Blackberry-Picking' and 'Twickenham Garden'. Even Rosenberg's 'Break of Day in the Trenches' is a lyric, despite its grim setting.

Hardy's poem fits both ways of thinking of a lyric. It is both a lyrical poem in its deeply personal, even lonely reflection, but also because it is shaped and rhymed exactly like a song. The rhymes are mostly very simple and easy to hear, although I admire *plume* and *gloom* and *outleant* and *lament*. They alternate, as does the rhythm, so that lines of eight syllables alternate with lines of six, evenly stressed throughout in what is known as a ballad form, but which, if you want to get really stark prosodic naked, consists of iambic tetrameter alternating with iambic trimeter. (Lines with four stressed syllables followed by lines with only three that are stressed.) Ballads go back a long way in England and other European countries, but they actually vary a lot in terms of their rhyme and rhythm. Most are much longer than this poem and they tend to tell a story too, so to know that 'The Darkling Thrush' is a ballad is less useful than to know how its form affects the way we react to it. The same is true of all prosody, the detailed, formal study of sound and rhythm in verse. You can identify a poem as a villanelle or an alexandrine if you like, count the number of anapaests or dactyls per line, but how that enhances your pleasure in it, what exotic chemicals it packs into the firework display it sets off for you is anyone's guess.

In the early days of our current digital dalliance, I remember someone using computers to analyse hundreds of sound recordings of performances by great concert pianists. They argued that what made these pianists great was the way they broke away from strict musical notation. The infinitesimally longer pause here or a minutely shorter demisemiquaver there, a more hasty *rallentando* or sticky *glissando* were all that distinguished them from ordinary, run-of-the-mill ivory-ticklers. When you read a lot of poetry and study it closely, you find something very similar. It is where poets break away from the basic model, when they break the rules that they are often most effective and interesting.

Hardy conjures up an especially bleak prospect for us at the start of this poem. His frost isn't silver or shining, it's *spectre-grey* and this is the *dregs* of winter. All of Hardy's writing is weighed down with rural tradition and life, so ghosts don't even raise an eyebrow, never mind a hair on the back of his neck. He doesn't offer us a Christmas cardi to keep out the cold or cheer the spirits. We don't even get a chirpy robin in the snow. The first intimation of sound comes from *The tangled bine-stems scored the sky/Like strings of broken lyres*, which is as elegant an image as one could ask for from any poet. It combines sight and sound through that clever pun on *scored*, which allows us to see the dark silhouettes of dead vines cut into the blank winter canvas of this *darkling* sky at the same time as we hear the wind playing a musical score through them. The lonely, meditative tone is enforced by Hardy's assertion that the evening is so inhospitable, *all mankind that haunted nigh/Had sought their household fires.* And in keeping with the *spectre-grey* frost, even the locals who might otherwise be outside working are thought of as ghosts, haunting. This really is a dismal and desperate view he invites us, through his eyes, to see and, strangely, to enjoy.

If you think that opening is joyless, verse two takes the comfortlessness to a whole new, wrist-slitting level of dismal. All that sharp clarity created by the *darkling* light seems to Hardy to turn what he sees from that gate into the personified corpse of the entire preceding century, laid out dead in front of him. The sky above becomes *His crypt* and the wind in those *tangled bine-stems* thrums out his *death-lament*. Life itself, *The ancient pulse of germ and birth*, is *shrunken hard and dry*, as Hardy himself gives in to the same, bewildering sense of an ending. If you read this poem carelessly, rush it or fail to inject something of yourself into it, don't be surprised if you don't get much out, if the firework fizzles to a faint red glow before a disappointing silence. You will miss the pulse embedded in the rhythm of that short line *The ancient pulse of germ and birth*. You will miss the way the 'd's in *hard and dry* clash so effectively with the 's's of *Was shrunken* that immediately precede them. All Hardy's poetic grace and subtlety will glide by you, wasted. Read it with focus and concentration, but most of all with a desire to appreciate and enjoy it, and you will find far more than is offered in this short essay.

At the end of the second verse, when Hardy's *fervourless*-ness reaches rock bottom, he hears a thrush singing in the branches of a tree above him. This is where that breaking of the rules, that slight shift in expectations has the most effect, and the insistent ballad rhythm that has dominated the poem so far gives way to four lines that flow unbroken, mimicking the small bird's expansive, joyful song.

> *At once a voice arose among*
> *The bleak twigs overhead*
> *In a full-hearted evensong*
> *Of joy illimited;*

It's easy to underestimate today how significant music was in Hardy's life. His father and grandfather were key members of a small group of musicians who played regularly at the local church. Hardy himself played the violin and in his eighties was able to remember songs and dances from his youth in complete detail. It's been almost two decades since American media theorist Neil Postman issued his prescient warning that 'culture always pays a price for technology'.[1] The impact a series of new technologies have had on the musical lives embedded in countless rural communities for centuries is not difficult to appreciate. Hardy wrote about it himself in his 1872 novel *Under the Greenwood Tree*, where the arrival of a new barrel organ renders the village choir redundant.

Exuberant, joyful singing by ordinary men and women was something Hardy was familiar with from almost every aspect of rural life, church, field and marketplace. The purity and simplicity he hears in the thrush's song might not be easy to access by a generation more familiar with the saccharine songsters of

Saturday-night television talent shows. There is no joy or value in spontaneity where songs are mere commodities. The recent revival of interest in choirs and choral singing may well have something to do with this. Hardy's scruffy little old thrush, *frail, gaunt, and small*, belting its heart out into the freezing winter air, isn't an entertainment. The miracle Hardy finds in this otherwise insignificant, isolated incident is that the bird *Had chosen thus to fling his soul/Upon the growing gloom*. And *soul* is not a word a writer like Hardy deploys lightly. Study Hardy seriously, and in many ways what you will find yourself quickly embroiled in is one man's lifelong struggle with his religious faith, or lack of it. In today's interminable trawl for TV talent, *soul* has a less gripping meaning.

The specifically Christian context 'The Darkling Thrush' relies on for effect is there in the bird's *evensong* and *carolings*. A highlight of the year for the Mellstock Quire in *Under the Greenwood Tree* is their tour of the local villages on Christmas Eve, singing carols at one neighbour's door after another, walking for miles, whatever the weather. Such well-trodden, arduous rituals are driven by faith, and the question the *ecstatic* thrush forces Hardy to ask, why, in such surroundings, does it sing like this? is no less substantial.

Like Ted Hughes and Seamus Heaney, Hardy's bond with nature is a vital part of his art. What shocks and provokes him leaning on that *coppice gate* is the striking difference between the thrush and every other component part of the natural world he is so used to observing. All of his senses tell him that the world has come to a bleak and dismal conclusion. He uses the word *terrestrial* as a scientific way of indicating his overpowering sense that all life has ceased, that the century's corpse is stretched out cold and dead in front of him.

Yet this one small creature reads things very differently. The thrush is neither cowed nor dulled by the cruel conditions. It refutes all the evidence, sweeps it away and sings with the kind of pure, unalloyed joy we naturally associate with spring or summer. Why? Hardy finds only one answer, but it matters so much it determines the poem, concludes it and leaves us, like the poet, full of preponderant thought.

> *I could think there trembled through*
> *His happy good-night air*
> *Some blessed Hope, whereof he knew*
> *And I was unaware.*

There is another poem by Hardy, which, once you're aware of it, invites comparison with 'The Darkling Thrush'. In 'The Oxen' Hardy retells a childhood story about how country folk believed that on Christmas Eve at midnight, all the farm animals would kneel down in their stables in remembrance of Christ's birth. He ends that poem by imagining himself going to see with his own eyes if it were true, knowing it to be nothing more than *fancy*, but *Hoping it might be so.* That same *Hope* inspired him in December 1900, the nagging doubt of an educated, intelligent Victorian whose Christian faith and upbringing has been painfully exposed by Darwin's *Origin of Species*, but whose lived experience teaches him altogether different lessons.

The Darkling Thrush

I leant upon a coppice gate
    When Frost was spectre-grey,
And Winter's dregs made desolate
    The weakening eye of day.
The tangled bine-stems scored the sky
    Like strings of broken lyres,
And all mankind that haunted nigh
    Had sought their household fires.

The land's sharp features seemed to be
    The Century's corpse outleant,
His crypt the cloudy canopy,
    The wind his death-lament.
The ancient pulse of germ and birth
    Was shrunken hard and dry,
And every spirit upon earth
    Seemed fervourless as I.

At once a voice arose among
    The bleak twigs overhead
In a full-hearted evensong
    Of joy illimited;
An aged thrush, frail, gaunt, and small,
    In blast-beruffled plume,
Had chosen thus to fling his soul
    Upon the growing gloom.

The Darkling Thrush

So little cause for carolings
    Of such ecstatic sound
Was written on terrestrial things
    Afar or nigh around,
That I could think there trembled through
    His happy good-night air
Some blessed Hope, whereof he knew
    And I was unaware.

Seventeen

The Rime of the Ancient Mariner
(1798)
Samuel Taylor Coleridge (1772–1834)

Far too lengthy to reproduce here, few poems become so famous that their characters escape the tight shackles of poetic metre to enter the wider public consciousness, or lines from them become idiomatic English. Coleridge's Ancient Mariner, like Lewis Carroll's Alice or Arthur Conan Doyle's Sherlock Holmes, is the kind of character who gets lifted and dropped unceremoniously into other people's stories. There's a good chance you may never have even read the poem but, nonetheless, you will have come across an image of a tattered old sailor with a huge, dead albatross strung round his neck somewhere. These few words from the chapped lips of Coleridge's weathered sea dog have earned a life of their own: *Water, water, every where,/Nor any drop to drink.* Coleridge's lengthy, undoubtedly unusual poem has led otherwise sensible people to credit the opium he was addicted to with its fantastic imagery, but that's the way with weakness – it often seeks to exploit others' strengths.

Coleridge was a philosopher, a theologian of sorts as well as a poet, and his writing about other people's writing, most notably Shakespeare's, has probably had far more impact on our culture than this weird and otherworldly poem about a sailor who kills an albatross. It featured in the famous collection of poems called *Lyrical Ballads*, published jointly with William Wordsworth in 1798 and which precipitated the entire Romantic movement at the precise moment in European history when the French were opting to pursue very similar ideals to do with individual freedom and liberty via a mechanical device that removed people's heads efficiently and in a suitably crowd-pleasing manner.

By now you should be used to the idea that any poet I introduce you to will arrive with some curious personal baggage. Coleridge comes with his own wardrobe and that of several travelling companions. He was never physically strong and emotionally was clearly as hard to stomach, as the opium he relied on to manage his poor health had some famously unpleasant side effects, besides depression. There is a hilarious moment in John Mortimer's play *A Voyage Round my Father* when he asks his father if he ever took opium. His father denies doing so, indignantly asking if his son has never seen a portrait of Coleridge whose sickly appearance he puts down to chronic constipation, though in far less clinical terms. If the history of English poetry was captured like the events on the Bayeux Tapestry, Coleridge's relationships with William Wordsworth and with Wordsworth's sister Dorothy, and the time he spent in the Lake District with them would stitch up a whole section all of its own, it was that important.

Together, Wordsworth and Coleridge set out to do something

consciously and deliberately new with poetry. Both were, in a sense, idealists. Coleridge allied himself with the poet Robert Southey in an entirely serious venture to set up a new and better kind of utopian society in America they called a Pantisocracy, which sounds like an innovative e-commerce business focusing on knickers and socks for the discerning business woman. It really means equal government by all and is a good illustration of Coleridge's inherently radical nature. He was dissatisfied with the world he inhabited and had that, at least, in common with Wordsworth. Like Blake, both men flirted with French revolutionary ideas but were too squeamish. I guess the thought of those mountains of heads endeared them to England as much as the mountains they loved to climb in the Lakes.

Lyrical Ballads was consciously experimental. Both poets disliked what they saw as poetry that was too far removed from most people by the language and techniques it used. Many of the *Lyrical Ballads* are about uneducated, rustic country folk and in Wordsworth's own words they use the 'real language of men', which is sleight of pen for an easier vocabulary. One of the questions I'll leave you to decide for yourself is how far *The Rime of the Ancient Mariner* lives up to that ideal. And it isn't simply a question of whether or not the mariner's use of *averred*, *gossameres* or *sultry* matches the ideal. It's a question that exposes the premise on which this entire book is written. If all you do is use simpler words, does it follow that more people will get the point of poetry?

I've read *The Rime of the Ancient Mariner* far too many times even to guesstimate, but before writing this essay I read it again, because Coleridge's poem is a little like a great short story: best enjoyed at one sitting. The mariner's *ghastly tale* is meant to be gripping, as the unlucky wedding guest finds out, and once started, don't expect to break for tea and a ship's biscuit. Not even *the feast*, or *the loud bassoon* being played by a *merry minstrelsy* is enough to wrench the wedding guest from the mariner's *glittering eye* or the steely grip of *his skinny hand*. That *bassoon* is a rare thing in great poetry: a rhyme so forced you can hear it squeal. The line Coleridge needs a rhyme with is *Till over the mast at noon*— and once he'd committed himself to *For he heard the loud . . .*, although a mandolin or hurdy-gurdy were never going to cut it, a *bassoon* just sounds downright eccentric, as though these minstrels included a wind player from the Berlin Philharmonic, moonlighting.

The poem tells such a rambling, singular story, it's difficult to write about it without summarising what happens, but since everything about it is weird, that's no easy task. So here is my attempt at a tweet. Sailor kills kindly albatross for no reason. Two hundred fellow shipmates die, but he survives to tell the tale, endlessly.

Hamlet's 'There are more things in heaven and earth, Horatio,/Than are dreamt of in your philosophy' may be anathema to writers like Richard Dawkins, but for Coleridge, Wordsworth and the ordinary men they were so concerned about, it hardly needed saying. *The Rime of the Ancient Mariner* wanders in and out of the natural and the spiritual world like a hippy backpacker with no compass but a bag full of mushrooms. Coleridge weaves a number of specific spirits into the tale, including one belonging to the ice and snow, who punishes the entire crew for the death of the albatross and who appears to control and torment the ship for months. The mariner sees two spirits aboard a ghost ship – whom he names *Death* and *Life-in-Death* – gambling with dice to decide his own fate, and two unnamed spirit voices have float-on parts later on in the poem, but appear to be too busy to hang around for much longer than to gossip. The two hundred dead men even turn into a *seraph-band* as the decrepit ship finally makes its home port, something the mariner calls *a heavenly sight!* All of these characters illustrate the poem's fascination with spirituality, and at times that spirituality is undoubtedly overtly Christian. Before he wakes after the albatross has fallen from his neck, the mariner prays, *To Mary Queen the praise be given!/She sent the gentle sleep from Heaven,* and several times he appeals to *Christ* in desperation as well as name. When the sailors first encounter the albatross they give it the respect due any other contemporary seafaring Englishman, *As if it had been a Christian soul,/We hailed it in God's name.* It's also an injustice to the poem to ignore the Christian symbolism the albatross itself carries in those immense, outstretched wings even before it gets killed for no reason then strung around the mariner's neck like a crucifix on a chain.

Even the natural world of the poem is otherworldly. Any geographical or meteorological accuracy on the ship's way to Antarctica is abandoned for eerie effect as wintery images like *ice, mast-high . . . floating by, As green as emerald* and *snowy clifts* are soon replaced by grotesques, *slimy things did crawl with legs/ Upon the slimy sea.* As a reader who naturally responds to poets who know about nature, I always find myself struggling with *the water-snakes* that finally trigger enough empathy in the mariner to pray.

> *I watched their rich attire:*
> *Blue, glossy green, and velvet black,*
> *They coiled and swam; and every track*
> *Was a flash of golden fire.*

It is in so many ways a vital moment in the story, the point when the mariner finally feels like a man again, which frees the albatross from his neck, yet the creatures that provoke his feelings are strange and unnatural. There is something unpleasantly Satanic and Miltonic about these particular water snakes, all gloss and glitter, but no fur coat. But I'm saving Milton for later, like decent champagne.

The Rime of the Ancient Mariner provokes different responses in different people. Some relish the poem's Romantic centrality, extrapolating from it whole theories about how we should live our lives, treat the planet we live on and, inevitably, the 'fellow' creatures we share it with. Others simply respond to its exotic story as they would to something from the *Arabian Nights* or Brothers Grimm. It's one of the most unpredictable fireworks in the box.

The part of the poem that understandably infuriates students new to it is the bit that fascinates me. At the point on their journey when they are most alone, when completely surrounded by ice that threatens to destroy them, when *Nor shapes of men nor beasts we ken,* the albatross glides into their lives, bringing nothing but pleasure and joy. They even feed it like a pet, *It ate the food it ne'er had eat,* before the ice suddenly *split with a thunder-fit* and *The helmsman steered us through!* With *a good south wind sprung up behind,* the albatross then stays with the ship, as these birds are well known to do in the lonely open ocean, *And every day, for food or play,/Came to the mariner's hollo!* Only then, without warning or even the slightest attempt at an explanation, the mariner shoots the bird with his crossbow, killing it.

> 'God save thee, ancient Mariner!
> From the fiends, that plague thee thus!
> Why look'st thou so?' With my cross-bow
> I shot the Albatross.

Students are often at a loss at what they see as this senselessly cruel act. All we get from Coleridge is the dramatic irony in the wedding guest's direct speech, his horror at the expression on the mariner's face as he reaches this critical point in the meandering tale he is forced repeatedly to tell. It comes as a question, *Why look'st thou so?* to which the answer is supremely matter-of-fact, superbly literal, *With my cross-bow/I shot the Albatross.* The horror is in his guilt.

No surprise that frustrates so many metropolitan students today. We have steadily and relentlessly removed sin from their lexicon. What Coleridge knew, amongst others, was the truth about nature and therefore about man. The mariner didn't *need* a reason. Man doesn't need his reason: just his will. Sitting where it does in the poetic timeline, *The Rime of the Ancient Mariner* speaks for its entire age, the Age of Reason. It poses the same question political theorist and founding father of the USA Thomas Paine laboured over in pages and pages of turgid prose. Knowing we have it, what use should we make of reason?

Famously, Coleridge always denied the poem had any kind of moral, even though the mariner offers up a pretty stark message at the end, which sounds very much as though it's been trotted out to thousands of innocent bystanders he has separated from the crowd, as he does with the wedding guest. When the poem was first illustrated by David Scott in 1837, Coleridge was baffled that Scott portrayed the mariner as an old man on board a ship, because in Coleridge's mind the mariner had only become *ancient* telling the tale many thousands of times, over many years, after the voyage. That Scott also portrayed the albatross as a cross between a pelican and a fat duck didn't seem to bother him as much.

> *I pass, like night, from land to land;*
> *I have strange power of speech;*
> *That moment that his face I see,*
> *I know the man that must hear me:*
> *To him my tale I teach.*

That tale always comes with a lesson, but before turning to that I want for a moment to dwell on that tantalising idea that the mariner selects his prey. There is something he recognises in the ones he stops. They *need* him. This is one of the loosest ends in all literature, as infuriating as Iago's determination to keep his mouth shut, after his malevolent manipulation of his master, Othello, has been revealed. Or the long, slow walk Anna Schmidt takes through falling leaves in a Vienna cemetery at the close of *The Third Man*. Coleridge gives us nothing to go on. The wedding guest is given few words to speak and nothing he says characterises him or suggests anything to identify him as one of those the mariner knows *must hear* him. But if you think of the alternative, of a poem in which the wedding guest is a distinct individual, someone we can see is targeted by the mariner because of something that distinguishes them from everyone else, from us – why bother with the lesson?

The lesson itself is simple and more than palatable to a modern readership literally well schooled in green politics and global warming. But before making his final pronouncement, the mariner takes a little detour that provides fertile fodder for professional academics. Returning to the party he pooped for the wedding guest, he uses it as a contrast.

> *O sweeter than the marriage-feast,*
> *'Tis sweeter far to me,*
> *To walk together to the kirk*
> *With a goodly company!—*
>
> *To walk together to the kirk,*
> *And all together pray,*

> *While each to his great Father bends,*
> *Old men, and babes, and loving friends*
> *And youths and maidens gay!*

The mariner offers completely conventional communal prayer, ordinary churchgoing if you like, as a *sweeter* choice than the worldly delights of the *marriage-feast*. It's easy in today's secular society to step over this inconvenient truth: that ordinary churchgoing was the norm for Coleridge and his readers, the spiritual everyday. Critics often prefer to make excuses for this part of the poem, discounting it as marginal. But it's there and it precedes the mariner's final few words of advice to the wedding guest.

> *Farewell, farewell! but this I tell*
> *To thee, thou Wedding-Guest!*
> *He prayeth well, who loveth well*
> *Both man and bird and beast.*
>
> *He prayeth best, who loveth best*
> *All things both great and small;*
> *For the dear God who loveth us,*
> *He made and loveth all.*

The biblical echoes would have been resounding for any reader of Coleridge's own era and merely because we are not churchgoers today, we shouldn't dismiss them. Hamlet could only say 'there is special providence in the fall of a sparrow' because

Shakespeare knew his audience understood the reference to Matthew's gospel. Coleridge knew his audience would identify the Garden of Eden far quicker than they would an albatross or an iceberg.

Wordsworth and Coleridge are often described as pantheists, religious and philosophical thinkers who see everything, every aspect of nature and the material world, as part of an all-encompassing, immanent God. God isn't external, separate from the natural world for pantheists. Both poets frequently write about the signs of divinity they observe with some awe in nature, but the mariner's lesson is a less radical one; his God is the sole creator of the Old Testament, *He made and loveth all.*

It's a challenge in today's patently secularised culture to learn anything from Coleridge's weathered old man. In a world where time itself is a mathematical, not a human experience, where we have designed astronomical instruments that let us see into time itself, he can so easily sound like a simpleton. In the first few pages of this book I argued that poetry operates on the edges of man's knowledge and experience, and centuries after its composition, *The Rime of Ancient Mariner* still does. Prayer is an unfashionable embarrassment to many who may never have faced adversity. It's striking how quickly 'ordinary men' of the twenty-first century faced with torment or terror resort to it, and there have been no shortage of events, natural and unnatural, to demonstrate this truth in recent times. Browse the mountains of flowers that appear at the scene of every tragedy and what you will find is a mass of small cards with handwritten prayers on them. The lurid balloons and cuddly toys that accompany some of them might clash with traditional views of what is a tasteful way to publicly signify grief. Like me, you might feel a little puzzled that so few of the generous givers remove any of the plastic wrapping that suffocates the natural beauty of all that blossoming, but it would be extraordinarily churlish to deny the generosity of their spirit or their desperate need to be heard. The Ancient Mariner's conclusion, *He prayeth well, who loveth well* sounds simply sensible in such circumstances.

Eighteen

The Eve of St Agnes
(1820)
John Keats (1795–1820)

Poetry is endlessly informative. I've been lucky enough to spend a substantial portion of my adult life studying it, yet it still surprises me, unlike politics. In the world of 'ordinary' women that Wordsworth, Coleridge and John Keats were all familiar with, St Agnes Eve was important because it was believed that by following a little ritual, young girls could get to see their future husbands. Keats's famous poem is constructed around this simple folk myth. One of the threads that has woven itself through these essays without my help is the habit poets have of resorting to the simple, the ordinary, folk myths and beliefs, things we might expect them to think uneducated. Donne yearns to be a mandrake root, Edith Nesbit pretends to be a wise country-woman steeped in near-magical knowledge, and even Hollie McNish adopts a contemporary vernacular because she feels her audience will feel more comfortable with it. If anything at all can be said to connect these poets, and so many others, it is a compulsive desire to communicate, to be heard. Few poets make money, even fewer a lasting reputation, yet they persist in this incredibly difficult, demanding art form that costs so much in terms of human effort and endeavour. However close their coterie, however narrow or knowing their circle or limited their print runs, poets are compulsive shouters, cat ladies on the bus who not only still have control of their senses, but senses more finely tuned than most of us.

The Eve of St Agnes will be difficult to enjoy unless you embrace it as the Gothic fantasy it was to Keats and remains today. It's been helped along the way, not least by the Pre-Raphaelites, who found equally intense pleasure in the same kind of fantasy, just in paint. Several members of the Brotherhood painted scenes from a number of Keats's poems, which have been widely reproduced. One reason I think they were drawn to it is because Keats has a vibrantly visual imagination. He takes time and trouble to describe things for you to see. Ironically, I don't think the Brotherhood do him justice. There is one painting by Holman Hunt of the *Eve of St Agnes* showing Madeline and Porphyro just about to escape, amidst a couple of sleeping drunks and dopey bloodhounds, which lives in the Guildhall Art Gallery in London. It seems more interested in the architecture than the lovers, and Porphyro's *lofty plume*, which early in the poem is to be found *Brushing the cobwebs*, looks more like a quill pen he hurriedly stuck in his cap, just in case he needed to leave her a note. Another by Millais in the Royal Collection shows Madeline undressing in the room and, considering the lengths Millais went to create it – his wife posed in the chilly moonlight for three nights and he used a professional model and a special lantern later to create the effect of moonlight through the stained-glass window – his Madeline is a frigid little madam. She stands half out of her ornate, heavy dress as though she's about to consult with a royal physician. I find myself asking if the view we're offered by Millais is through Porphyro's eyes, hiding in his closet, then I can see why it's a closet and not a wardrobe he's in. I can also see why he brought all those *cates and dainties* with him. She'll need something to keep her occupied. You'll find much more passion and delight reading the poem than in anyone's attempts to paint it.

The poem borrows heavily from *Romeo and Juliet*. The enmity between the lovers' feuding households is so fierce Porphyro risks his life being in Madeline's family mansion, and like Romeo, he is helped in getting access to her bedroom by a female member of her household, the Beldame Angela. But the core of the poem is that essentially voyeuristic, dramatic idea of Porphyro hiding in a closet while Madeline undresses for bed, knowing she is following the St Agnes Eve ritual, which will allow her to see her husband to be. The ritual takes various forms in the folksy, William Morris world of mead and maidens, but for Madeline it requires some specific steps, actions dictated to her by respectable *old dames full many times* and which Keats is at pains to make clear are also respectable, however erotic. Madeline's *heart had brooded, all that wintry day,/On love, and wing'd St Agnes' saintly care*, before she finally escapes the revelry for the devilry. The *saintly* ritual she has to follow denies her supper, which was probably wise, since Porphyro manages to secrete not just himself in the closet, but an almost absurdly exotic romantic dinner for two consisting of:

> *... a heap*
> *Of candied apple, quince, and plum, and gourd;*
> *With jellies soother than the creamy curd,*
> *And lucent syrops, tinct with cinnamon;*
> *Manna and dates, in argosy transferr'd*
> *From Fez; and spiced dainties, every one,*
> *From silken Samarcand to cedar'd Lebanon.*

That use of exotic, foreign names is something of a trademark in Milton, but even in hell, Milton simply can't compete with Keats for luxury and decadence. The sounds of these varied delicacies are as delicious as their imaginary flavours. Keats is a genius when it comes to creating effects from a list of things. The first and final verses of his ode 'To Autumn' are exquisitely beautiful examples, to be enjoyed some time after Madeline and Porphyro have left sleeping dogs lying.

Yet the ritual also places her in an extraordinarily vulnerable position, stretched out *supine* on her bed, without looking behind her or to either side, but only staring heavenwards. The single line, *And couch supine their beauties, lily white;* implies nakedness, as is common in the folk versions of the ritual, and it obviously adds a whole layer of eroticism and tension to the poem. This is what she must do to satisfy St Agnes.

> *They told her how, upon St Agnes' Eve,*
> *Young virgins might have visions of delight,*
> *And soft adorings from their loves receive*
> *Upon the honey'd middle of the night,*
> *If ceremonies due they did aright;*
> *As, supperless to bed they must retire,*
> *And couch supine their beauties, lily white;*
> *Nor look behind, nor sideways, but require*
> *Of Heaven with upward eyes for all that they desire.*

Although the adolescent wheeze of hiding in her wardrobe only hits Porphyro when he is talking to Angela below stairs, Keats stresses Madeline is game throughout and she is so intent on the St Agnes Eve opportunity that she dances and takes part in the festivities with the other 999 guests, barely noticing they are there.

> *The music, yearning like a God in pain,*
> *She scarcely heard: her maiden eyes divine,*
> *Fix'd on the floor, saw many a sweeping train*
> *Pass by—she heeded not at all:*

It's worth appreciating at this point the version of the poem Keats preferred and wanted to publish is lost. The poem we enjoy today is not the one he wanted us to enjoy. He wrote a version in which Porphyro and Madeline enjoyed a sexual, as well as a gastronomic blowout in her bedroom, before eloping past the drunks and dozy bloodhounds onto the stormy moors at night.

His publisher John Taylor and their mutual friend Richard Woodhouse advised against it on the obvious grounds of decency and that it would offend female readers. They won and Keats's preferred fantasy vanished for ever, but the discussion that took place between them throws an unusually bright spotlight onto male sensibilities of the period. The following is from Woodhouse's letter to Taylor.

> *But, as it is now altered, as soon as M. has confessed her love, P. winds by degrees his arm around her, presses breast to breast, and acts all the acts of a bona fide husband, while she fancies she is only playing the part of a wife in a dream. This alteration is of about 3 stanzas; and tho' there are no improper expressions but all is left to inference, and tho' profanely speaking the Interest on the reader's imagination is greatly heightened, yet I do apprehend it will render the poem unfit for ladies.*[1]

In his reply, Taylor makes it clear he's not interested in publishing the poem if it contains the offending stanzas. Woodhouse also reports Keats as having told him:

> *that he should despise a man who would be such an eunuch in sentiment as to leave a maid, with that Character about her, in such a situation: and should despise himself to write about it, &c &c &c, and all this sort of Keats-like rhodomontade.*[2]

It's clear Woodhouse and Taylor shared a view that there was something of the prima donna about Keats, but Keats's passionate, eunuch-phobic sentiment, as well as his opinion of Madeline's 'Character', certainly get my approval, even though he acquiesced and went along with Taylor's wishes. Keats creates an erotic appetite in Madeline's bedroom that not even his exotic comfort food can sate.

For Keats's readers sex was about marriage, families and love. We live in times quite alien to that sensibility and it may be difficult for some readers to really grasp the idea that sex was a physical act bound tightly in people's minds to marriage and a lifelong commitment to family life. If your willing suspension of disbelief is unwilling to entertain the idea that Madeline and Porphyro's love for each other draws them into that bedroom, then it's unlikely the poem will strike you as dramatic.

Keats is so aware of this connection, so incapable of thinking otherwise, that the poem is packed with religious imagery that purifies both Porphyro's and Madeline's natural desires, setting them clearly inside the confines of a marriage blessed in heaven, however dreadful it is to Madeline's kin, whose sleep is troubled with nightmarish visions.

> *That night the Baron dreamt of many a woe,*
> *And all his warrior-guests, with shade and form*
> *Of witch, and demon, and large coffin-worm,*
> *Were long be-nightmar'd.*

Despite Keats's complaints, it's hard to imagine his three missing stanzas would get even the most censorious vicar's wife hot under the squalor. When he first arrives outside Madeline's mansion, Porphyro *implores/All saints to give him sight of Madeline*, and again it is to the saints he turns when Angela expresses her disapproval of his plan to hide in the closet, '*I will not harm her, by all saints I swear,*' he promises. When he finally wakes Madeline up, not with a kiss, but by playing her own lute close to her ear, he drops to his knees instantly and silently at her bedside, like a religious statue, *Upon his knees he sank, pale as smooth-sculptured stone.* The most voyeuristic moment in the entire poem, when Madeline kneels as she enters the room and the moonlight through the stained-glass window casts a red, heraldic light onto the pale skin of her breasts, is couched not in *supine* or *lily white* beauty, but in relentlessly religious terms:

> *Full on this casement shone the wintry moon,*
> *And threw warm gules on Madeline's fair breast,*
> *As down she knelt for heaven's grace and boon;*
> *Rose-bloom fell on her hands, together prest,*
> *And on her silver cross soft amethyst,*
> *And on her hair a glory, like a saint:*
> *She seemd a splendid angel, newly drest,*
> *Save wings, for heaven:—Porphyro grew faint:*
> *She knelt, so pure a thing, so free from mortal taint.*

In case it still needs spelling out, Madeline is a saint, not a sinner, an angel, not a whore.

The closest we get to any kind of physical or emotional consummation between these two lovers comes when Madeline reacts to the sight of her stony lover by pleading with him to wake up and warble again, *Give me that voice again, my Porphyro,/ Those looks immortal, those complainings dear!* The change is immediate. Licensed by Madeline, Porphyro obeys and stands, transformed and godlike.

> *Beyond a mortal man impassion'd far*
> *At these voluptuous accents, he arose*
> *Ethereal, flush'd, and like a throbbing star*
> *Seen mid the sapphire heaven's deep repose;*
> *Into her dream he melted, as the rose*
> *Blendeth its odour with the violet,—*
> *Solution sweet: meantime the frost-wind blows*
> *Like Love's alarum pattering the sharp sleet*
> *Against the window-panes; St Agnes' moon hath set.*

Keats offers a demanding combination of imagery to convey what is essentially a conventional, even fairy-tale experience: that moment when a couple embrace, physically and emotionally acknowledging they love one another for the first time. He asks us to juggle two similes, that *throbbing star* and *the rose* blending its scent with a violet, while simultaneously balancing on the metaphor *into her dream he melted* that unites the two. Then he resolves all doubt with a new, alliterative metaphor, *Solution sweet*, and the forceful caesura that follows it. Contrasting with all this passion, the stanza ends with evidence of the winter night outside and the ominous sound of *sharp sleet*, striking the window *Like Love's alarum* before another caesura in the middle of the final line signals it's time we turned our eyes respectfully elsewhere, because anything our vivid, Pre-Raphaelite imaginations might have indulged in is over, *St Agnes' moon hath set*.

The remainder of the poem sees Madeline briefly voice every literary virgin's post-coital fear, the thought that Porphyro will now abandon her, before Porphyro affirms not just his love but his determination to marry her, suggesting eloping there and then is the best way to ensure their mutual happiness. It's all a bit of a climb down, if not the elastic one Romeo enjoys under Juliet's balcony as they both battle with the mere thought of being apart. However dramatic or covertly erotic we might find *The Eve of St Agnes* when we read it, it's a poem that ends on a bleak and daunting note. Keats makes good use of his skill with lists, and besides the nightmares experienced by Madeline's father, *the Baron ... And all his warrior-guests,* we're told *The Beadsman* and *Angela the old* are long since ashes. Keats brings his readers out of his fantasy to the present day with a jolt: *And they are gone: ay, ages long ago/These lovers fled away into the storm.* It's a clever trick because it doesn't matter whether the reader is his contemporary, ours or enjoys the poem in some unknown future. Madeline and Porphyro are always well and truly dusted as well as done. For a poem about love, *The Eve of St Agnes* makes a very poor love poem.

Love remains a popular subject for poets of all sexual tastes because the best of them do work at the very boundaries of man's knowledge and experience, plus neither neuroscience nor psychology has added much to the sum total of our knowledge about this universally significant human phenomenon.

Keats, like Coleridge, admired Shakespeare. He even imagined him as the muse behind his poem *Endymion* and famously claimed he possessed a quality that has kept undergraduates downing an excess of late-night coffee for decades, 'negative capability', which, trust me, for any coffee-drinking undergraduates reading, is merely the ability to value effect above logic.

While writing this essay I was lucky enough to see a Royal Shakespeare Company production of *Venus and Adonis*, Shakespeare's lengthy narrative poem and probably his first full work. Lucky. because it's rarely read by anyone, never mind performed professionally. The hour-long production consisted of a classical guitarist, a narrator and five puppeteers who had created a performance using techniques based on Japanese Bunraku puppetry. The puppets were about a third human size and were manipulated by hand; the puppeteers, dressed all in black, were visible, just very discreet. It was beguilingly charming, a magical blend of poetry, music and astoundingly graceful, credible movement. Besides a couple of horses and an impressively aggressive wild boar, the only characters are Venus and Adonis, but what impressed me most of all was the beauty and fluency of the poetry. Being part of that audience required no effort at all. There was none of the focus on actors, character or action the plays demand. The whole thing felt like the most pleasant kind of dream, those rare ones when you wake up just wishing you could turn over and instantly return to the world you were in, and recover those delightful feelings you know you just left, sleeping.

Where practical, in most of the preceding chapters I've managed to provide you with a copy of the poem concerned to read and enjoy at the chapter's end. *The Eve of St Agnes* has forty-two verses and is well over half the length of *The Rime of the Ancient Mariner*, but taking a lesson from the poets themselves, I'm going to break that rhythm for what I hope are not just practical, but good reasons.

In *Venus and Adonis*, Venus succeeds, after a literally superhuman effort, in seducing Adonis who, obsessed with hunting, tells her frankly and pointedly he is only interested in a different kind of game. The RSC's 2017 production brought out the humour inherent in this particular skirmish between the sexes beautifully, Venus's passion for him butting up against Adonis's passion for hunting, as well as making much of her own puppet butt, repeatedly. But what I found most memorable and crucially, given the aim of this book, useful was the declaration Venus makes about love, after Adonis has been killed by the wild boar. It is the climax of the poem and I've reproduced it here for you to read and enjoy as it stands. It is one great poet's thoughts on love and if anyone – psychologist, philosopher, cleric or mystic – has done a better job of capturing at one go all the baffling complexity of this quintessentially human experience, I have yet to see or hear it.

From *Venus and Adonis*
by William Shakespeare

'Since thou art dead, lo! here I prophesy,
Sorrow on love hereafter shall attend:
It shall be waited on with jealousy,
Find sweet beginning, but unsavoury end;
Ne'er settled equally, but high or low;
That all love's pleasure shall not match his woe.

'It shall be fickle, false, and full of fraud,
Bud and be blasted in a breathing-while;
The bottom poison, and the top o'erstraw'd
With sweets that shall the truest sight beguile:
The strongest body shall it make most weak,
Strike the wise dumb and teach the fool to speak.

'It shall be sparing and too full of riot,
Teaching decrepit age to tread the measures;
The staring ruffian shall it keep in quiet,
Pluck down the rich, enrich the poor with treasures;
It shall be raging mad, and silly mild,
Make the young old, the old become a child.

'It shall suspect where is no cause of fear;
It shall not fear where it should most mistrust;
It shall be merciful, and too severe,
And most deceiving when it seems most just;

Perverse it shall be, where it shows most toward,
Put fear to valour, courage to the coward.

'It shall be cause of war and dire events,
And set dissension 'twixt the son and sire;
Subject and servile to all discontents,
As dry combustious matter is to fire:
Sith in his prime Death doth my love destroy,
They that love best their love shall not enjoy.'

Nineteen

The Bistro Styx
(1995)
Rita Dove (1952–)

I came across 'The Bistro Styx' by the American poet Rita Dove completely by accident, but it immediately caught my ear. Even the title is an invitation to think, a clever culture clash in two tiny words. Most people will know the River Styx as the river dead heroes cross to reach Hades in Greek mythology, usually with the help of the ferryman, Charon, thrusting out his skeletal hand to demand payment. The word 'bistro' has strayed well beyond its Parisian origins, but to most people still means an inexpensive restaurant with an aversion to fast food. Combining the two implies a genial night out before death.

The poem does indeed make you think, and Dove issues an invitation, not a threat. One of the poems competing for my attention with 'The Bistro Styx' at the time of writing was a famous poem by Philip Larkin, 'Church Going', written in 1955. Larkin, a librarian by nature as well as for tax purposes, was never the kind of poet to issue threats, but when I read it again recently, 'Church Going' seemed, about sixty years after its composition,

The Bistro Styx

to be one of the most poignant and prescient poems I have ever read. In it he describes wandering into a silent church and then predicts the future we all now inhabit. He pictures the church overrun with weeds and grass, empty, obscure, growing gradually more and more unrecognisable week by week through disbelief as much as disinterest.

There are two such churches within five minutes walk from where I live now. One, an attention-seeking arts centre I can't bring myself to set foot in, the other an unrecognisable stone box with buttresses, paved in weed and brambles. However, it's what edged Larkin out and Dove in that interests me, because both poems repay the reader tenfold.

Poets lose control the moment their work is published. We all bring something of ourselves to a poem. Poetry is a joint venture and in 'Church Going' and 'The Bistro Styx' I feel strangely like a majority investor. Both poems address me, personally, in ways many of the poems I've shared here already simply can't. Trench warfare defeats my taste for horror, which is non-existent anyway, and Gothic fantasy has never been my cup of glee. But raw, human, lived experience, thought about and thought through, the kind that catches you by the heart as much as by surprise, always makes me sit up and pay attention. I like it when a poet's life feels like mine.

I've wandered into many churches, in search of something, sometimes just solitude, sometimes art, often inspiration and, at times, God. I've had my fair share of bistro pleasures, even Parisian, so I can *relate to* these two poems.

But that isn't why I like them both or why I opted to share

'The Bistro Styx' with you. It's the thinking they require that I most admire. Unlike so many artists with an agenda, Dove and Larkin don't just understand it's a joint venture; they expect your commitment to it. They want you to think for yourself, not think like them.

'The Bistro Styx' is set in a Paris bistro, and draws us to join a meeting between a mother and her daughter, the mother a visitor, the daughter a *nouvelle parisienne* reluctantly accepting this invitation to dine on her new turf. The mother is alone until her daughter appears and we are given her point of view throughout; it is her narrative voice that makes us think. The daughter is, in the probable words of the mother, shacked up with a local artist but the mother's disapproval stings audibly through words she has to stifle instead of share.

> *'How's business?' I asked, and hazarded*
> *a motherly smile to keep from crying out:*
> *Are you content to conduct your life*
> *as a cliché and, what's worse,*
>
> *an anachronism, the brooding artist's demimonde?*

She goes on to describe her daughter's business in scathing terms.

> *Near the rue Princesse they had opened*
> *a gallery cum souvenir shop which featured*
> *fuzzy off-color Monets next to his acrylics, no doubt,*

> *plus bearded African drums and the occasional miniature gargoyle from Notre Dame the Great Artist had carved at breakfast with a pocket knife.*

That italicized *cum* and the capitalised *Great Artist* show Dove isn't afraid of using the niceties of grammatical convention to make a point. Great poets know that the arsenal the English language offers them is both extensive and refined. Both these dainty uses of grammar groan under the weight of irony. The daughter's business is neither gallery nor souvenir shop, her boyfriend neither great nor an artist. Mother knows best.

Students studying the poem have somewhere latched on to a parallel with the Greek myth about Demeter and Persephone, as though that alone *explains* things. Stuck in the Styx, they search for connections, picking out one detail here, another there that they believe reflects the Greek myth, as though that in itself were a valuable activity. It's a sad indictment of the way poetry is so often taught and indicative of why I wrote this book. However aware Dove herself may have been of that parallel when writing the poem, she doesn't and can't make it part of some deal the reader must buy into. It's up to you what you bring to the poem.

There's one particular metaphor that I think exposes this delightfully. The mother is acutely aware of the way her daughter has dressed for this occasion: *she was dressed all in gray,* she observes, before detailing specific items of her clothing, nailing each particular shade of grey with a painter's eye. Later she can't help herself voicing her sense of pride, *She did look ravishing,* but initially, she regards her daughter's appearance as indicative of *the brooding artist's demimonde* role she is playing to perfection. That first impression ends up as this metaphor, as she sits back in her chair to look harder at *my blighted child, this wary aristocratic mole*. The labyrinthine efforts students make to try and *explain* that burrowing little image would make me feel sorry for them if I wasn't standing here holding that sparkler. Moles are near-blind, incessantly mobile creatures, all pink nose, twitching whiskers and sleek, iron-blue, *grey* coat. That the daughter is also *aristocratic* only seems fair in Paris, a city defined by riches and revolution. I can see this girl because of Dove's poetic talent. Whether or not Dove drew the same connections when opting for *mole* or whether the meaning of *mole* in the internecine world of espionage also entered her mind really doesn't figure. It's the reaction it sparks in me and you that matters, the ideas that erupt from that joint venture. I see this girl clearly and distinctly. I know her better for that metaphor, sense her mother's sadness more as a result.

And it is a sad poem, a genial encounter before dying. As the daughter tucks greedily into the food, relishing one clichéd French course after another, Chateaubriand, Camembert, her mother watches quietly and knowingly, finally essaying the one thing she has wanted to know all night, '*But are you happy?*' Barely acknowledging the question, the daughter invites her mother to appreciate the fruit she is busy gorging herself on, and however much mythologically inclined students might wish it, pomegranates aren't on the menu. Nonetheless, the mother knows this is a kind of death. *I've lost her, I thought, and called for the bill.* I have brought up two daughters without the help of their mother, so although I doubt either of them is likely to fall for a daubing depressionist and move to an arty Paris suburb, I know that bistro chair waits for me.

With its echoes of Demeter and Persephone, 'The Bistro Styx' highlights one of the reasons why so many adult readers still avoid poetry. Referencing other poets is a powerful weapon in the poets' armoury. I've already pointed out how dependent on other literature all writing is, but when poets make open or even covert references to other works, they signal something that lots of people find off-putting: cleverness. Poets know their art is extraordinarily condensed, that their job is to pack meaning into those few words. Using myths, images, even just names from the past is efficient, poetic shorthand. We've seen Carol Ann Duffy do this effectively in her poem 'Mrs Midas' in chapter eight. It happens anyway, whether poets choose to do it or not. You can't drop the words 'rose' or 'thorn' into a poem without spilling a bit of blood. Some words tread lightly, others come in hobnailed boots. None arrive without a history. When poets like T. S. Eliot and Milton make extreme and conscious use of their predecessors, they cultivate an aura of scholarship around them that less-well-read people understandably find irritating or even opaque.

It's a double-edged sword, which if this book is doing the job it was designed to do, you may well have noticed is an anagram of 'words'. The price poets like Milton and T. S. Eliot pay for their use of other writers is fewer readers. Which is why they shout louder on the bus. My advice is that you should never worry about what you don't know, or rush, like Rita Dove's students, to look things up in the hope of finding an explanation. Your part of the bargain is to bring yourself to the poem, no more than that. Venture that much and a great poet will rarely disappoint you. I enjoy 'The Bistro Styx' not because I know lots about classical mythology from studying poetry, but because I'm a dad who loves his daughters.

Bringing yourself to the poem is an idea worth exploring, because if you read a poem in the same way so many people troop through contemporary art galleries, strolling past installations and paintings in a kind of semi-conscious submissiveness, you'll leave equally empty-headed. Unlike so many contemporary artists, whose egos are more glaringly on display than their work, poets like Dove and Larkin actually care about you. That's why they write to you.

That act of coming to the poem with an open mind is like listening to someone, sincerely and carefully, paying attention to the words they use, the ideas those words convey and what effect they have on you. It's the equivalent in that gallery of stopping to gaze at the canvas in detail. To take in the use of colour, of light and shade, of all the skills the artist needed to create that amazing image hanging isolated on a wall in front of you. It starts with humility and admiration, the knowledge that not everyone can do that. It helps to apply the same principle to poetry. A canvas a chimpanzee has thrown paint at can sell for thousands. I'm still waiting for one to spell 'eek!'

The Bistro Styx

She was thinner, with a mannered gauntness
as she paused just inside the double
glass doors to survey the room, silvery cape
billowing dramatically behind her. *What's this,*

I thought, lifting a hand until
she nodded and started across the parquet;
that's when I saw she was dressed all in gray,
from a kittenish cashmere skirt and cowl

down to the graphite signature of her shoes.
'Sorry I'm late,' she panted, though
she wasn't, sliding into the chair, her cape

tossed off in a shudder of brushed steel.
We kissed. Then I leaned back to peruse
my blighted child, this wary aristocratic mole.

'How's business?' I asked, and hazarded
a motherly smile to keep from crying out:
Are you content to conduct your life
as a cliché and, what's worse,

an anachronism, the brooding artist's demimonde?
Near the rue Princesse they had opened

a gallery *cum* souvenir shop which featured
fuzzy off-color Monets next to his acrylics, no doubt,

plus bearded African drums and the occasional miniature
gargoyle from Notre Dame the Great Artist had
carved at breakfast with a pocket knife.

'Tourists love us. The Parisians, of course'—
she blushed—'are amused, though not without
a certain admiration . . .'
The Chateaubriand

arrived on a bone-white plate, smug and absolute
in its fragrant crust, a black plug steaming
like the heart plucked from the chest of a worthy enemy;
one touch with her fork sent pink juices streaming.

'Admiration for what?' Wine, a bloody
Pinot Noir, brought color to her cheeks. 'Why,
the aplomb with which we've managed
to support our Art'—meaning he'd convinced

her to pose nude for his appalling canvases,
faintly futuristic landscapes strewn
with carwrecks and bodies being chewed

The Bistro Styx

by rabid cocker spaniels. 'I'd like to come by
the studio," I ventured, "and see the new stuff.'
'Yes, if you wish . . .' A delicate rebuff

before the warning: 'He dresses all
in black now. Me, he drapes in blues and carmine—
and even though I think it's kinda cute,
in company I tend toward more muted shades.'

She paused and had the grace
to drop her eyes. She did look ravishing,
spookily insubstantial, a lipstick ghost on tissue,
or as if one stood on a fifth-floor terrace

peering through a fringe of rain at Paris'
dreaming chimney pots, each sooty issue
wobbling skyward in an ecstatic oracular spiral.

'And he never thinks of food. I wish
I didn't have to plead with him to eat . . .' Fruit
and cheese appeared, arrayed on leaf-green dishes.

I stuck with café crème. 'This Camembert's
so ripe,' she joked, 'it's practically grown hair,'
mucking a golden glob complete with parsley sprig
onto a heel of bread. Nothing seemed to fill

THE POINT OF POETRY

her up: She swallowed, sliced into a pear,
speared each tear-shaped lavaliere
and popped the dripping mess into her pretty mouth.
Nowhere the bright tufted fields, weighted

vines and sun poured down out of the south.
'But are you happy?' Fearing, I whispered it
quickly. 'What? You know, Mother'—

she bit into the starry rose of a fig—
'one really should try the fruit here.'
I've lost her, I thought, and called for the bill.

Twenty

The Sea and the Skylark
(1877)
Gerard Manley Hopkins (1844–1889)

I never planned it this way, but this book risks turning into *Poems for Twitchers*. It began with George Mackay Brown's 'The Hawk', embraced the song of blackbirds in Edward Thomas's 'Adlestrop' before meeting Hardy's 'The Darkling Thrush' and soaring off with Coleridge's albatross. But the reason I chose 'The Sea and the Skylark' by Jesuit priest and Victorian poet Gerard Manley Hopkins is because he represents a real hike in difficulty. No surprise from a member of an organisation often thought of as the Pope's intellectual storm troopers. Jesuits are also renowned for their self-abnegation, so I suppose historically, Pope Francis, the first Jesuit to be made commander-in-chief is a through-the-looking-glass version of Donald Trump: capitalist ignoramus made president.

'The Sea and the Skylark' is a Petrarchan sonnet, fourteen lines following a clear rhyming pattern you can discover for yourself, but the conventional shape of such a sonnet into a verse of eight lines followed by one of six (octet then sestet) is usually changed by editors into two verses of four lines, followed by two of three (quatrains followed by tercets), which, although 'tercet' sounds like a bird, is just a verse three lines long. Fourteen lines doesn't take up much space on a page, but these are fourteen of the most surprising, unorthodox combinations of words and sounds you are likely to find on the page of any book that isn't written in code.

Hopkins is such a unique poet; many readers new to him find his verse baffling, even impenetrable. Hopkins thought originality was non-negotiable. To be a great poet you had to be one of a kind. He certainly achieved that. A perfect poem was supposed to be 'beautiful to individuation' which the critic W. H. Gardner helpfully explains: 'By which he probably meant "beautiful to the point of bringing out all the complex individuality of the subject, which includes, in effect, the individuality of the artist".'[1]

But that's taking a very academic route I've managed to avoid. Instead let's stick to the meandering, hopefully less muddy path I've led you down thus far, because if you thought the private lives of some of the earlier poets we've looked at were complicated, they were a dry and dull walk in the park compared to Hopkins. Brought up in a large and talented, high-Anglican family, he gained a reputation as a rebellious but gifted pupil at Highgate School, was a talented draughtsman, an outstanding classicist at Balliol College, Oxford, who chose religion instead of poetry (he burned all his early poems), upsetting all his family by converting to Catholicism and not just that, but by choosing to become a Jesuit. He spent the last years of his life as a university lecturer in Dublin, teaching Latin and Greek, but life choices had estranged him from his own nation as well as his large family, which meant he was often lonely and even depressed. This all combines to make him an easy target for psychoanalysis. Choose a hang-up and someone will hang it on Hopkins. Although writing things like this in letters to friends is just inviting students with all the etymological discernment of a tabloid sub-editor to run riot: 'Now it is the virtue of design, pattern, or inscape to be distinctive and it is the vice of distinctiveness to become queer. This vice I cannot have escaped.'[2]

Once you embrace the unorthodox nature of Hopkins's verse, the deliberate artiness of it, and hear what he's really interested in, you will quickly find he was a man in love with the natural world. To say nature inspired him is a bit like saying Falstaff enjoyed a drink or the Marquis de Sade a bit of spanking.

Hopkins looked for and found his God in almost anything that wasn't manufactured. Trees, stars, the sea, a kestrel, a kingfisher, trout, cows, swimmers (and famously non-swimmers); his poems are riddled with riddles religiously inspired by aspects of nature he saw around him. Yelling from that top deck of the bus in the opening lines of one of his poems he proclaims: *'The world is charged with the grandeur of God./It will flame out like shining from shook foil'*. One of the crucial mistakes I think many unsupported readers of poetry make is not taking poets seriously enough. They hear statements like this one from Hopkins as passing thoughts or just observations. Be in no doubt; Hopkins believed this just as Milton believed that, by writing *Paradise Lost*, he could *'assert Eternal Providence,/And justifie the wayes of God to men'*.

Biographers date 'The Sea and the Skylark' to the year of Hopkins's ordination, 1877, and to a specific Welsh coastal town, Rhyl, because he was studying theology at St Beuno's College near St Asaph in North Wales. Never one to waste time, Hopkins taught himself Welsh while there, and experts in prosody have investigated how Welsh poetry influenced his own experiments with metre. Interesting though that all is, Hopkins is far from one of those poets – we've met several already – who consciously creates a poetic persona. Poetry was too important for that kind of Byronic vanity. He abandoned it for the priesthood and only took it up again after years of abstinence, when asked by a fellow Jesuit to commemorate a maritime tragedy that became his famous poem 'The Wreck of the Deutschland'. That poem is a lengthy, overtly Christian ode about a shipwreck that drowned 157 poor souls, including five Franciscan nuns who had been forced to leave Germany by anti-Catholic legislation aimed initially at expelling the Jesuits. The poem wasn't published until 1918. Very little of Hopkins's work was ever seen by anyone before his death. It's intriguing that so many great poets really are largely unknown and unread until they've been punting with Charon on the River Styx.

One of Hopkins's great strengths is he rarely wastes time on anything. The poem starts with two distinct sounds coming from different directions, *On ear and ear, two noises too old to end* a line that looks deceptively simple, but by now I hope you have quickly spotted is actually meticulously constructed around the use of internal rhymes. As a quick illustration of just how impressive this kind of artless artfulness is, ask yourself how easily could you write a line of poetry, ten to twelve syllables long with a caesura in the middle, internal rhymes in each half, and ending with a half-rhyme: *ear* and *ear*, *two* and *too*, *old* and *end*. Then remember that you have to rhyme the last word of the first line, *end*, with the last word of the fourth line; in this case Hopkins chooses *wend*. With that challenge in mind, here is the first verse in its entirety for you to see how he maintains that pattern to differing degrees in subsequent lines.

> *On ear and ear two noises too old to end*
> *Trench—right, the tide that ramps against the shore;*
> *With a flood or a fall, low lull-off or all roar,*
> *Frequenting there while moon shall wear and wend.*

Believe it or not, it's a single, grammatically perfect sentence even dimwitted computer software doesn't throw wiggly green lines at, yet when you first see or hear it, I suspect for most people the density and complexity of both sound and meaning are quite daunting. I studied Hopkins many years ago as a student and learned a little trick then that is invaluable, although it sounds almost inane. When you read any poem by Hopkins, trust absolutely to his punctuation but crucially, exaggerate it a tiny bit. Try it with that first verse and see what I mean.

It will immediately force you to read across the first to the second line (enjambment) and come to a sudden halt after *Trench*, which makes what otherwise sounds like a really odd word act as he wants it to, because it's a verb here, not a noun. The two noises *Trench*, and if you trench something, you cut into it, making some sort of impression on a flat surface. Hopkins's poetry is full of curious word usages, old words resurrected, compound words made with hyphens, even completely new coinages, when I assume he felt disappointed by the dictionary. Punctuation is often the perfect key to meaning in Hopkins, because he was so well read and educated that a misplaced comma would have felt like a grain of sand in his eye.

So *Trench* in this first verse suddenly carries significant meaning as well as aural force. These two sounds, which turn out to be the sea and the lark song, make a profound impression on him. They arrest him and force him to contemplate what he hears. Alone on this fairly wild Welsh shoreline, Hopkins is listening to the voice of God.

I could easily devote pages and probably provide you with a stultifying experience if I were to explore in detail all the various techniques Hopkins uses to convey to us these two particular sounds – sea and skylark – in the next four lines. The second verse is dedicated to trying to capture their essential beauty, exactly as they captivated Hopkins himself on that day over 150 years ago, something he calls in his writings 'inscape'. More pages could easily be wasted explaining where he got this idea (the medieval theologian Duns Scotus) and how he refined it, but by now I'm optimistically assuming it will be far more enjoyable and productive to let you exercise your own skills and sensibility on his verse. So here is that second verse for you to recapture Hopkins's own experience that day on the Welsh coast. Because that is why he wrote it for you.

Left hand, off land, I hear the lark ascend,
His rash-fresh re-winded new-skeinèd score
In crisps of curl off wild winch whirl, and pour
And pelt music, till none's to spill nor spend.

There's little point running a survey to find listeners' top one hundred favourite pieces of classical music in the UK. Ralph Vaughan Williams's *The Lark Ascending* will inevitably come top. I once lay flat out on the grass for half an hour with my two young daughters, the three of us just looking up into an absurdly blue June sky at skylarks singing. Now in their teens, every so often they remind me of that afternoon, it made such a deep impression...

If you know what a skylark sounds like as it spirals slowly upwards until it becomes almost impossible to see with the naked eye, you will almost certainly find Hopkins's four lines impressive, because through them he somehow manages to evoke that extraordinarily lyrical, unmistakable music. The author George Meredith, whose 1881 poem 'The Lark Ascending' inspired Vaughan Williams in 1914, takes about sixty-four out of 122. If you don't know what a skylark sounds like – and I absolutely appreciate that many readers really will not have a clue, not least because they aren't native to North America – the simplest thing to do is find an online recording, rather than trust to Vaughan Williams's rendering, musical genius though it is.

But it isn't simply the unusual beauty of their song that makes the lark a favourite with poets. Wordsworth, Isaac Rosenberg, Ted Hughes and Christina Rossetti are just a few of the poets who have found inspiration from these small brown birds with their comical headgear. Their association with rural life runs deep. They are early risers and because of that are associated with the dawn, although you will hear them singing at any time of the day. Their song is continuous and lengthy, much longer than most birds, their spiralling flight upwards and down before they plummet abruptly to earth is spellbinding and they nest on the ground, which makes their eggs and chicks vulnerable. Larks have a range of clever strategies to disguise themselves or divert predators from their nests, and even where I live, which is not thirteen miles from central London, I have seen them fluttering barely off the ground, as though wounded, because I or my hairy best friend, a Border terrier called Toast, have inadvertently strayed too close to their nest. There is a lot to think about in a lark.

Those two natural sounds Hopkins hears, the surge of the surf and the song of the lark, are set starkly against the nearby town, presumably Rhyl, which he turns to contemplate for the final two verses of the poem. *How these two shame this shallow and frail town!* he exclaims, and in doing so he reaches across 150 years to encourage us to acknowledge possibly the single most important question confronting all of us today.

The question relies on our response to that one word, *shame*. If you can't understand why that would be so, then it's going to be difficult for you to follow Hopkins's thought. He knows that's a risk and tries to help by explaining, *Being pure,* the sea and the skylark *ring right out our sordid turbid time.* Their purity lies in their being, like man, created by God. Rhyl is undoubtedly and strikingly man-made. The skill and aptness of that internal rhyme, *sordid* and *turbid,* are remarkable and you can see how experimental Hopkins is in that inventive phrase, *ring right out,* not a combination you're likely to see elsewhere, but one that works. As a Christian and a Jesuit you would expect Hopkins to reflect his belief that man is made in God's image so this idea, *We, life's pride and cared-for crown,* isn't likely to surprise us as much as what follows it: *Have lost that cheer and charm of earth's past prime:* we are no longer like the sea or the skylark, pure.

Those two words, *cheer* and *charm* are so suited to the sentiment, the argument, and yet so perfectly in harmony with the poem's sound and metrical structure, it's quite poignant to see how reluctantly Hopkins entertained the idea that his own talent was equally an expression of 'God's Grandeur', the title of another of his most famous poems. In a letter to the Reverend R. W. Dixon he wrote:

When a man has given himself to God's service, when he has denied himself and followed Christ, he has fitted himself to receive and does receive from God a special guidance, a more particular providence. This guidance is conveyed partly by the action of other men, as his appointed superiors, and partly by direct lights and inspiration. If I wait for such guidance, through whatever channel conveyed, about anything, about my poetry for instance, I do more wisely in every way than if I try to serve my own seeming interests in the matter.[3]

'The Sea and the Skylark' asks us to contemplate the stark difference between the world God created and the one mankind has created. Man's impact on the only planet we inhabit is rarely out of the news today, whether in terms of climate change, technology or social and political conflict. I can easily see why some contemporary readers might baulk at Hopkins's Christian faith, but this isn't a theological question and Hopkins never insists it is. The words he chooses, *charm* and *cheer*, *dust* and *slime*, offer us a clear choice, not a compromise.

Most of us today inhabit cities or towns. I've worked long enough in education to know that many thousands of schoolchildren live their entire lives along a narrow path between home and school, in their bedrooms, on small screens and rarely, if ever, stray outside of a local geographical space you could swing a particularly stretchy cat in. What chance do they have to grasp Hopkins's choice? If you have no opportunity to wonder at the natural world, no wonder you don't value it. It's an observation William Wordsworth made as long ago as 1805 in his poem *The Prelude*, which is the subject of the next chapter.

Not long ago I spent about six months working in London's Canary Wharf, which for all its wealth and economic aspiration is a just collection of immense glass boxes, clustered around vast troughs of water collecting litter brought there by idleness and fierce winds generated by the tall buildings. However hard I tried to get a physical sense each day, on the short walk from tube station to office – to look up at the sky, appreciate the drizzle on my face or the sun reflecting on the water of the docks – these scraps of nature did little to raise my spirits or anything approaching the wonder I feel merely watching trees in a breeze. Religious faith has nothing to do with it. If you can't sense something greater than yourself from the prospect before you, life must feel like a difficult and harsh sentence.

One afternoon, returning to the office, I was standing speaking on my phone at the edge of one of the docks when a seal stuck his black, shiny, whiskery head right out of the water about three feet away. The shock was palpable. He dived, then came up again a little further away and then was gone. I was so delighted I looked around me to tell people on the street to look too. I couldn't wait to tell colleagues back at the office, and in truth was a little disappointed when one of them told me the seal was well known and even had his own website because he had learned to swim up to Billingsgate Fish Market, where employees threw him scraps of fish. Every day after that, whenever I had sight of a stretch of water, I looked out for him, but he never made another appearance, at least for me.

The poem ends with this bleak estimation of our cleverness and creativity.

Our make and making break, are breaking, down
To man's last dust, drain fast towards man's first slime.

That single most important question confronting us today, which 'The Sea and the Skylark' poses across decades, two world wars and technological and social change Hopkins would probably find terrifying, is how should we treat the world we inherit? It's a question as relevant to the lazy, after-hours office drinker who leaves their empty beer bottle by the side of the dock in Canary Wharf for someone else to kick into the dark water, as it is to the scientist who devotes their life to measuring man's impact on the natural resources of the earth or the politician responsible for deciding which laws to enact. Like all great poets, Hopkins challenges our thinking through the intricacy and sincerity of his.

The Sea and the Skylark

On ear and ear two noises too old to end
Trench—right, the tide that ramps against the shore;
With a flood or a fall, low lull-off or all roar,
Frequenting there while moon shall wear and wend.

Left hand, off land, I hear the lark ascend,
His rash-fresh re-winded new-skeinèd score
In crisps of curl off wild winch whirl, and pour
And pelt music, till none 's to spill nor spend.

How these two shame this shallow and frail town!
How ring right out our sordid turbid time,
Being pure! We, life's pride and cared-for crown,

Have lost that cheer and charm of earth's past prime:
Our make and making break, are breaking, down
To man's last dust, drain fast towards man's first slime.

Twenty-One

The Prelude
(1805)
William Wordsworth (1770–1850)

It's time to bring out the big guns. The kind that jut skywards outside the Imperial War Museum like postmodern sculptures, or the one Rudyard Kipling's Kim sat on at the start of his epic journey.

Contestants on *Pointless*, a quiz show currently popular on British TV, are always hoping to find an answer to a question that no one, out of a hundred people asked, could produce. If asked to name any English poet, most competitors would avoid William Wordsworth like the plague because they know he would probably be one of the most common answers. His alliterative, lexical name is synonymous with poetry. Ask a child clutching a crayon to draw a picture of a poet and it will be William Wordsworth standing on those stick-thin legs smiling at you under spiky hair. We've mentioned him already when exploring Coleridge, and especially their joint enterprise, *Lyrical Ballads*, but besides a dalliance with a host of daffodils, his fame rests to a large extent on one lengthy, autobiographical poem, *The

Prelude. It's that poem which I'm going to invite you to read and enjoy. It comes, like almost everything good for you today, with a health warning. To read all thirteen books[1] of blank verse will probably take you about seven to eight hours of non-stop reading, about two or three days if you're holidaying close to a pool and a sun lounger.

It's essentially an autobiographical epic, years on an imaginary psychiatrist's couch compressed into one huge poem, so the obvious route in would be to tell you something about Wordsworth's life and background as I've done with earlier poets. But the whole purpose of this book has been to offer a better, personal, richer route to enjoying poetry than more downtrodden approaches. How poorly some of those approaches work became all too clear on National Poetry Day recently in an exchange in a national educational publication I write a column for, when another author suggested that perhaps schools weren't doing a great job of teaching poetry. He argued that 'learning how to write poetry seriously is not a subject suitable for a school curriculum'.[2] Outraged responses, worryingly from people actually being employed to teach poetry in schools, mostly shared a view that poetry is in some unique way free from any of the conventional constraints we rely on for language to be intelligible. One commentator made this child-friendly statement: 'Poetry affords people (not just students) the opportunity to express and communicate in all the colours of the rainbow.'[2]

In contrast, I've aimed throughout to treat all readers as adults and gradually ease you into having the confidence to take any poem at face value, to bring yourself, your own experiences, thoughts and ideas to the poem so that it can set off that firework display that makes poetry a unique reading pleasure. For that reason I'm going to give you the opening section of the poem to read and respond to for yourself, without any upfront guidance or interference from me. This is how *The Prelude* opens.

> *Oh, there is blessing in this gentle breeze,*
> *That blows from the green fields and from the clouds*
> *And from the sky; it beats against my cheek,*
> *And seems half conscious of the joy it gives.*
> *O welcome messenger! O welcome friend!*   5
> *A captive greets thee, coming from a house*
> *Of bondage, from yon city's walls set free,*
> *A prison where he hath been long immured.*
> *Now I am free, enfranchised and at large,*
> *May fix my habitation where I will.*   10
> *What dwelling shall receive me, in what vale*
> *Shall be my harbour, underneath what grove*
> *Shall I take up my home, and what sweet stream*
> *Shall with its murmurs lull me to my rest?*
> *The earth is all before me—with a heart*   15
> *Joyous, nor scared at its own liberty,*
> *I look about, and should the guide I chuse*
> *Be nothing better than a wandering cloud*
> *I cannot miss my way. I breathe again—*
> *Trances of thought and mountings of the mind*   20
> *Come fast upon me. It is shaken off,*

As by miraculous gift 'tis shaken off,
That burthen of my own unnatural self,
The heavy weight of many a weary day
Not mine, and such as were not made for me. 25
Long months of peace—if such bold word accord

With any promises of human life—
Long months of ease and undisturbed delight
Are mine in prospect. Whither shall I turn,
By road or pathway, or through open field, 30
Or shall a twig or any floating thing
Upon the river point me out my course?

Enough that I am free, for months to come
May dedicate myself to chosen tasks,
May quit the tiresome sea and dwell on shore— 35
If not a settler on the soil, at least
To drink wild water, and to pluck green herbs,
And gather fruits fresh from their native bough.
Nay more, if I may trust myself, this hour
Hath brought a gift that consecrates my joy; 40
For I, methought, while the sweet breath of heaven
Was blowing on my body, felt within
A corresponding mild creative breeze,
A vital breeze which travelled gently on
O'er things which it had made, and is become 45
A tempest, a redundant energy,

*Vexing its own creation. 'Tis a power
That does not come unrecognised, a storm
Which, breaking up a long-continued frost,
Brings with it vernal promises, the hope   50
Of active days, of dignity and thought,
Of prowess in an honourable field,
Pure passions, virtue, knowledge, and delight,
The holy life of music and of verse.*

*Thus far, O friend, did I, not used to make   55
A present joy the matter of my song,
Pour out that day my soul in measured strains,
Even in the very words which I have here
Recorded. To the open fields I told
A prophesy; poetic numbers came   60
Spontaneously, and clothed in priestly robe
My spirit, thus singled out, as it might seem,*

*For holy services. Great hopes were mine:
My own voice cheared me, and, far more, the mind's
Internal echo of the imperfect sound—   65
To both I listened, drawing from them both
A chearful confidence in things to come.*[3]

Whatever else strikes you about the speaker, this is a serious man harbouring serious thoughts. The *friend* he refers to here and throughout the poem, by the way, is none other than our own old friend Coleridge, and one of Wordsworth's aims in the poem is to sing his fellow poet's praises. Many of the most difficult passages of *The Prelude* are long sections in which Wordsworth thinks aloud in verse. He jokes at one point about having to be careful when he was walking his dog as a youngster, composing lines of poetry aloud as he walked, in case anyone saw him and decided he was mad. Facing all thirteen books, you should know *The Prelude* was always intended as just that, a prelude to a much greater epic poem, to rival Milton's *Paradise Lost*. Universities have educated many thousands of students who were probably deliriously happy to discover Wordsworth never actually got to write that epic after they had read *The Prelude*. There are far too many moments when the poem appears never to have been edited by a professional. When he writes, *Four years and thirty, told this very week,/Have I been now a sojourner on earth*, in Book VI, what he really means is he is thirty-four, and when he starts any line with *Oh!* I sometimes actually feel my spine contract.

It's poetry as endurance sport. It requires commitment and sustained effort, determination and, at moments, something akin to courage. There are huge passages in which we witness Wordsworth's mind at work, watch the cogs turn and the teeth engage as he tries to understand something he finds immensely difficult to grasp himself, before attempting to explain it to us. Sentences start off in one direction only to reach a crossroads Wordsworth can't resist exploring one path a time, before turning back to find the signpost again and pick up his original route.

They sometimes stagger under the sheer weight of words until the reader collapses exhausted, begging for a quick rest, while the poet strides on like a zealous rambler on amphetamines, lungs heaving, head bent into the teeth of some piercing gale towards a hilltop so distant that it's only visible for split seconds between banks of billowing grey clouds, only attainable after another arduous day of non-stop walking, as he screams into the wind, 'Keep up! Keep up!'

The opening passage is mercifully free of these, although the sentence beginning *Nay more . . .* at line 39 shows signs of rambling before he reins it in. It does, however, provide you with a perfect opportunity to practise something which will make *The Prelude* and, when you get there, Milton's *Paradise Lost* much easier to cope with, and much more enjoyable.

When looking at Hopkins I advised you to exaggerate his punctuation just a little. With Wordsworth, what you need to do is get used to thinking rigidly in terms of single sentences. Tell yourself that as you read, you will read one sentence at a time, as fluidly as you can and, most importantly, faster than might normally be considered polite. For some reason Wordsworth's verse seems to infect many who attempt to read it aloud with a kind of verbal narcolepsy. Far better to take each sentence at speed and then stop. And I mean stop. You will need to if you want to avoid endlessly rereading ideas you simply didn't grasp the first time. Try it now with the opening passage again and see how it feels. No, go on try it. I'm not going to reprint those sixty-seven lines of verse again just because you can't be bothered to turn back a page or two. Watch out for that inevitable full stop, exclamation mark or question mark and dig your heels in when it arrives.

Amazing, isn't it? Suddenly what might have at first seemed dense and difficult to follow opens up and becomes not just intelligible, but even pleasurable. Cambridge University's English faculty has produced an online resource[4] that contains all thirteen books of the 1805 version of the poem for you to read as scrollable text, while simultaneously listening to them being read aloud by different members of the faculty. It's fascinating to compare the various readings, how the readers approach the task, their tone and manner. Book VIII is read by a number of different voices and the variety in tone, confidence and skill is striking. It demonstrates just how difficult it is to read difficult poetry well.

Sophie Read's reading (how apt is that?) of Book IX is simply exemplary and illustrates perfectly how much a skilful reading of any poem can enhance our understanding, as well as our enjoyment of it. It is perfection. Even the most professional voiceover actress would not do any better. Her mastery of Wordsworth's sentencing is as audible as it is admirable. Embed this habit of thinking about and reading *one sentence at a time*, and even the most turgid, meandering sections of the poem will succumb to sense.

The following section from Book II highlights the nature of Wordsworth's sentencing perfectly. Read it as I advised, and you will find it is one huge sentence, so unwieldy it almost comes crashing down, followed by one that is admirably concise, done and dusted in one line, and only seven words.

> *The seasons came,* 310
> *And every season to my notice brought*
> *A store of transitory qualities*
> *Which, but for this most watchful power of love*
> *Had been neglected, left a register*
> *Of permanent relations, else unknown,* 315
> *Hence life, and change, and beauty, solitude*
> *More active, even, than 'best society',*
> *Society made sweet as solitude*
> *By silent inobtrusive sympathies,*
> *And gentle agitations of the mind* 320
> *From manifold distinctions, difference*
> *Perceived in things, where to the common eye,*
> *No difference is; and hence, from the same source*
> *Sublimer joy; for I would walk alone,*
> *In storm and tempest, or in starlight nights* 325
>
> *Beneath the quiet Heavens; and, at that time,*
> *Have felt whate'er there is of power in sound*
> *To breathe an elevated mood, by form*
> *Or image unprofaned; and I would stand,*
> *Beneath some rock, listening to sounds that are* 330
> *The ghostly language of the ancient earth,*
> *Or make their dim abode in distant winds.*
> *Thence did I drink the visionary power.*[4]

Popular neuroscience will tell you, like crows and lots of other similarly creative and cultured creatures, Homo sapiens can only hold about seven items in our short-term memory. The whole idea of what constitutes a short-term memory and how it connects with our long-term memory remains in dispute, but I'm perfectly willing to believe seven is about right. I struggle to do any two things at once routinely, such as driving and speaking even hands free on the phone, for example, or making supper and discussing with my daughter the Byzantine relationships of her 'squad'. So I actually think fans and teachers of difficult poetry like Wordsworth dramatically underplay how complex an issue poetic sentencing really is. There is a kind of discipline-wide denial about this from the literati. It's partly that unpleasant clique issue again: 'Of course anyone with half a brain could understand! I can: can't you?' Well, even a cursory examination of the passage I've just cited contains, I estimate, thirteen separate concepts, interdependently constrained within the one, lengthy sentence. I'm not the least surprised people find this kind of verse not so much tender, as tough.

I hope you are beginning to suspect that reading *The Prelude* can be a strikingly ambivalent experience. It has never surprised me that anthologists and teachers tend to select the most dramatic sections of the poem to reproduce, whether for enjoyment or for the demands of the exam syllabus. The poem sways from profoundly difficult, abstract concepts, passages in which Wordsworth is worrying his own thoughts aloud, to beautifully rendered descriptive passages, often of places or events that made a deep impression on the young poet. The latter are simply more accessible to most readers. So that section in Book I when, as a boy, he steals a small boat and rows out across Ullswater in the moonlight and watches a cliff face rising menacingly above the trees, before hurrying back to the shore, guilt-ridden, is a favourite choice.

Another dramatic section, from Book IV, though less frequently reproduced, describes how he met a soldier by the roadside who was walking to his home village after recently returning from abroad and leaving the army. The entire passage is so well written, even in blank verse. Wordsworth transports you into the past to stand beside him, like an imaginary childhood friend, as he tries to negotiate this awkward encounter with a forbidding stranger through youthful kindness and humanity. It's like looking at a landscape painting by Meindert Hobbema or John Martin and suddenly changing places with one of those small human beings standing beside a rutted country lane. The account of how the young and fit Wordsworth somehow manages to guide the exhausted, hardened, experienced veteran to a nearby cottage for food and somewhere to sleep is as poignant as it is timeless. In Book VIII, describing his time in London, he stops to have what James Joyce would have called an epiphany, and draws the scene so well that I, for one, can see this painting as though it's been hanging in a favourite room in the National Gallery for years.

In the tender scenes
Chiefly was my delight, and one of these
Never will be forgotten. 'Twas a man,   *850*

Whom I saw sitting in an open square
Close to the iron paling that fenced in
The spacious grass-plot: on the corner-stone
Of the low wall in which the pales were fixed
Sate this one man, and with a sickly babe   855
Upon his knee, whom he had thither brought
For sunshine, and to breathe the fresher air.
Of those who passed, and me who looked at him,
He took no note; but in his brawny arms
(The artificer was to the elbow bare,   860
And from his work this moment had been stolen)
He held the child, and, bending over it
As if he were afraid both of the sun
And of the air which he had come to seek,
He eyed it with unutterable love. [5]   865

Similarly, there is a description of street life in Book VII, *Residence in London*, which provides the kind of insight into daily life that historians, with their dependence on more formal documents, must sometimes crave. The 1805 London streets Wordsworth invites you to join him in are nothing if not cosmopolitan.

Briefly, we find (if tired of random sights,
And haply to that search our thoughts should turn)   235
Among the crowd, conspicuous less or more
As we proceed, all specimens of man
Through all the colours which the sun bestows,

And every character of form and face:
The Swede, the Russian; from the genial south,   240
The Frenchman and the Spaniard; from remote
America, the hunter Indian;
Moors, Malays, Lascars, the Tartar and Chinese,
And Negro ladies in white muslin gowns.[6]

This isn't the only surprise *The Prelude* springs. It's a bold poem. It's subtitled *Growth of a Poet's Mind* and by now, having touched on the lives of twenty successful poets, it's clear that anything seeking to describe what goes on in a poet's skull is headed for dark and deep water. Wordsworth qualifies this subtitle himself helpfully towards the end of the poem when he refers to it as *the history of a poet's mind.*[7] Wordsworth was a key voice in a far wider Romantic movement that abjured traditional authority in favour of individual freedom. The French Revolution, which he so admired and geographically as well as actively sought to align himself with, gave that voice a lasting political emblem, yet some of the most tight-lipped sections of *The Prelude* are those that cover his time spent in Paris, and elsewhere in France, during the revolution. One short extract, early in Book IX, captures this characteristic well. Like naughty tourists everywhere, he can't resist a bit of sly pilfering, and lifts a chunk of the now ruined Bastille as a souvenir. But the act itself provokes this intriguing reaction.

Where silent zephyrs sported with the dust
Of the Bastille I sate in the open sun

> *And from the rubbish gathered up a stone,*   65
> *And pocketed the relick in the guise*
> *Of an enthusiast; yet, in honest truth,*
> *Though not without some strong incumbencies,*
> *And glad—could living man be otherwise?—*
> *I looked for something which I could not find,*   70
> *Affecting more emotion than I felt.*
> *For 'tis most certain that the utmost force*
> *Of all these various objects which may shew*
> *The temper of my mind as then it was*
> *Seemed less to recompense the traveller's pains,*   75
> *Less moved me, gave me less delight, than did*
> *A single picture merely, hunted out*
> *Among other sights, the Magdalene of le Brun,*
> *A beauty exquisitely wrought—fair face*
> *And rueful, with its ever-flowing tears.* [8]   80

The unremarkable Magdalene concerned is exhibited in the Louvre today. Although her tear-filled eyes are artful enough, the rest is just an excess of drapery and a louring sky. Wordsworth's anecdote is maddeningly abstruse even when you consider a lump of stone is never likely to put more of a lump in your throat than a beautiful painting. It does, however, make me smile to think how many lumps of the Berlin Wall must lie in sock drawers or underneath small piles of neatly folded underwear all over Europe today. Perhaps, like bits of the 'true Cross', if you gathered them all together you'd have enough to reconstruct the wall twice over.

There is a brief moment in Book X when he appears to acknowledge his own reluctance to deal with the brutality of revolution, instead of the theory.

> *I crossed—a black and empty area then—*
> *The square of the Carousel, a few weeks back*
> *Heaped up with dead and dying, upon these*
> *And other sights looking as doth a man*
> *Upon a volume whose contents he knows*   50
> *Are memorable but from him locked up,*
> *Being written in a tongue he cannot read,*
> *So that he questions the mute leaves with pain,*
> *And half upbraids their silence.* [9]

It's a perfect example of how poets think and work, underscoring the central argument that has sustained this entire book about the point of poetry. Acutely aware of his own feelings, Wordsworth's only way of describing them to others, of conveying what is essentially an emotion, is through imagery and, specifically, metaphor. And look at just how complex that metaphor is, how dependent it is on connecting its various component parts. It risks ruining the effect, but the point I'm eager to make is fundamental and too significant to pass by. The Place du Carrousel, recently the site of the guillotine but now empty of decapitated bodies and the demonic contraption used to disassemble them, appears to him like a book he knows is significant, but which he can't read because it's written in a language he doesn't know. The phrase *locked up* reminds us that valuable books were often physically contained by a locking mechanism or chained to library desks. The pages are silent, *mute leaves*, which frustrate and even anger him in spite of his knowing that his own linguistic limitations are the reason for his lack of understanding. Not an easy thought for modern students taught that access to knowledge is dependent more on their teachers than themselves. And by the time you've reached this point in the poem, after discovering so much about his near-feral childhood, his fierce bond with nature, the ambiguity in his use of that innocent little word *leaves* is frankly, thumping.

Yet ask yourself, does this successfully communicate what he felt? How satisfactory is it as an explanation for his apparent failure to address the horror and inhumanity? How different is it from the 'we were just following orders' defence offered by many on trial at Nuremberg? No wonder that later, in Book X, he returns to this theme with an intensity of self-scrutiny it is painful to listen to. Wordsworth's soul-searching about the rights and wrongs of the French Revolution are at times so frank and awkward, the reader is tempted to look away, as though the words on the page will burn.

Lured and led by evolutions in technology that have taken place far too fast for politicians or lawmakers to keep pace, in a predominantly secular age, we have concluded that the language of science is essentially the same thing as truth. Ironically, it's in the language of the courtroom, not the language of the laboratory, where words take their most brutally naked form. However eloquent some barristers might think they are, the language of the law is the polar opposite of the language of poetry. In commercial negotiations I have watched lawyers quibble and dissect single words tirelessly in search of financial gain, however small.

This potent belief that science equals truth is the undisputedly dominant intellectual conviction of the age.

In Book II of *The Prelude*, addressing Coleridge directly, Wordsworth makes this very point himself about science and about how poetry works in comparison, about why it matters.

> *Thou, my Friend! art one*
> *More deeply read in thy own thoughts; to thee*
> *Science appears but, what in truth she is,*
> *Not as our glory and our absolute boast,*
> *But as a succedaneum, and a prop* 220
> *To our infirmity. Thou art no slave*
> *Of that false secondary power, by which,*
> *In weakness, we create distinctions, then*
> *Deem that our puny boundaries are things*
> *Which we perceive, and not which we have made.*[10]

Science, then, is just another man-made delusion, a *succedaneum*, a replacement for the real thing: poetry. Strange as it may sound, I believe him.

In his book *The Blind Watchmaker*, Richard Dawkins, who perhaps more than any other modern writer exemplifies the openly unholy alliance between science and secularism, says this:

It is raining DNA outside. On the bank of the Oxford canal at the bottom of my garden is a large willow tree, and it is pumping downy seeds into the air ... It is raining instructions out there; it's raining programs; it's raining tree-growing, fluff-spreading algorithms. That is not a metaphor, it is the plain truth. It couldn't be any plainer if it were raining floppy discs.[11]

This is, of course, a lie. As I look out of my study window, it is indeed raining. Every inch of visible sky is the colour of duct tape, I can see clear drops of water as they strike the paving stones, and the wet grass, which needs mowing, is going to have to wait. It is raining.

The point is that simply saying *this is not a metaphor* doesn't make it so. Dawkins *is* using rain as a metaphor and like so many scientists and, indeed, researchers in every imaginable field, he uses it, resorts to it and completely relies on it whenever thought becomes difficult, because Wordsworth is right and language is the only tool, with the exception of maths, he has in his toolbox.

One of the most annoying aspects of my day job these last few years, when I have been reading a lot of research, is how often an entire argument relies on nothing more than metaphor. It's not unusual in my field, educational research, to find a team of researchers – often really lobbyists working for a think tank or NGO – who design a research project on preconceived notions, then draft a lengthy paper which, however many figures or colourful illustrations and graphs it contains, ultimately relies entirely on metaphorical language to assert its 'findings'. In a work of art – a novel, play or poem – figurative language, often metaphor, is something we have a right to expect, admire and hope may even enlighten us. In the practical, pragmatic world of science and active social research, it's just a sign of weak methodology.

Nonetheless, our contemporary tendency to separate science as empirical and true from art, which is imaginative and based on fantasy, is a weakness of the age, a signal to history of how impoverished we are. In healthier cultures, poetry has always explored what language is capable of and people have engaged with it intellectually because it empowers us to live richer, livelier lives. One of many moments in *The Prelude* when Wordsworth rolls up his sleeves and shows us why he is the one name, amongst so many, synonymous with this demanding art form, is in Book VIII. Returning to London, he wants to make us understand how he felt at the very moment he realised he was entering the city again, sitting on top of *an itinerant vehicle* of some kind, surrounded by *vulgar men*. The realisation almost overwhelms him, *A weight of ages did at once descend/Upon my heart*, but what most impresses me is the intensity of the metaphor he uses to convey to us that feeling, the astounding skill involved in putting it together.

> *As when a traveller hath from open day*
> *With torches passed into some vault of earth,*
> *The grotto of Antiparos, or the den*
> *Of Yordas among Craven's mountain tracts,*   720
> *He looks and sees the cavern spread and grow,*

Widening itself on all sides, sees, or thinks
He sees, erelong, the roof above his head,
Which instantly unsettles and recedes—
Substance and shadow, light and darkness, all 725
Commingled, making up a canopy
Of shapes, and forms, and tendencies to shape,
That shift and vanish, change and interchange
Like spectres—ferment quiet and sublime,
Which, after a short space, works less and less 730

Till, every effort, every motion gone,
The scene before him lies in perfect view
Exposed, and lifeless as a written book.
But let him pause awhile and look again,
And a new quickening shall succeed, at first 735
Beginning timidly, then creeping fast
Through all which he beholds: the senseless mass,
In its projections, wrinkles, cavities,
Through all its surface, with all colours streaming,
Like a magician's airy pageant, parts, 740
Unites, embodying everywhere some pressure
Or image, recognised or new, some type
Or picture of the world—forests and lakes,
Ships, rivers, towers, the warrior clad in mail,
The prancing steed, the pilgrim with his staff, 745
A mitred bishop and the throne'd king—
A spectacle to which there is no end.[12]

I acknowledge, besides the considerable difficulty we've already highlighted around short-term memory and the complex sentencing, this may be a challenge for readers who have never entered a cave. If you have never felt that curiously unfamiliar sensation of being under the earth, not on it, of being gripped on all sides by darkness so solid you daren't move against it in case it pushes back at you, this metaphor is going to leave you a bit in the dark. How light, any light transforms that kind of underground environment is where Wordsworth's beautiful metaphor starts. Fortunately I've visited both the Carlsbad Caverns in New Mexico and the Neja caves in southern Spain, so the imaginative effort involved is a lot easier. I once visited a gypsum mine in the UK and the guide turned off all the lights. I don't think I'd enjoy the imaginative games Milton plays with darkness half so much if he hadn't.

So significant is poetry, that Wordsworth believes it capable of transforming mankind itself, outstripping earth itself as a divine creation.

> . . . *what we have loved*
> *Others will love, and we may teach them how:*
> *Instruct them how the mind of man becomes*
> *A thousand times more beautiful than the earth*
> *On which he dwells, above this frame of things*   450
> *(Which, 'mid all revolutions in the hopes*
> *And fears of men, doth still remain unchanged)*
> *In beauty exalted, as it is itself*
> *Of substance and of fabric more divine.*[13]

Separated from the natural world, man is an alien on his own planet. It's a theme we have seen echoed repeatedly by the poets featuring in these essays, not because of any conscious design or choice on my part, but because it is there in poetry throughout the ages. *The Prelude* voices this concern most clearly in Book XII, where Wordsworth's liberal politics are most evident and, not unsurprisingly given everything we have noted about the part be believes poetry plays in any society, the idea is presented to us as an unquestionable truth.

> *True it is, where oppression worse than death*
> *Salutes the being at his birth, where grace*   *195*
> *Of culture hath been utterly unknown,*
> *And labour in excess and poverty*
> *From day to day pre-occupy the ground*
> *Of the affections, and to Nature's self*
> *Oppose a deeper nature—there indeed*   *200*
> *Love cannot be; nor does it easily thrive*
> *In cities, where the human heart is sick,*
> *And the eye feeds it not, and cannot feed:*
> *Thus far, no further, is that inference good.*[14]

City living is as detrimental to human happiness, to love, as grinding poverty, a thought I can't imagine making it onto the agenda of any meeting between modern housing officials and architects in cities today, whether in Manchester or Mumbai.

However you wish to stare at it, *The Prelude* is a remarkable cultural asset. Like Shakespeare's plays, the paintings of J. M. W.

Turner or the music of Ralph Vaughan Williams, there is something immutably English about it. English literature as an academic discipline is well named because so often the objects of study have an umbilical connection to the culture of the English portion of the British Isles, not just the language. If it has any weakness, it is one Wordsworth is himself aware of. He devotes many pages and many hundreds of words to describing his childish and youthful connection with the natural world not just as an account but as a kind of psychological self-analysis. So intense is this effort that he confides in Coleridge, as well as with us:

> *Thus the pride of strength,* 70
> *And the vain-glory of superior skill*
> *Were interfus'd with objects which subdu'd*
> *And temper'd them, and gradually produc'd*
> *A quiet independence of the heart.*
> *And to my Friend, who knows me, I may add,* 75
> *Unapprehensive of reproof, that hence*
> *Ensu'd a diffidence and modesty,*
> *And I was taught to feel, perhaps too much,*
> *The self-sufficing power of solitude.*

That *perhaps too much* is the closest you will get anywhere in the poem to serious doubt, but it's a doubt that has resonance today, not least because of the shift of whole populations into cities. Cosmopolitan life hasn't eradicated loneliness. Solitude cultivates self-sufficiency, not society.

Within five minutes of having written what I thought was the close to this chapter, I heard a radio programme discussing how a huge increase in urban single households had changed eating habits, largely for the worse. An executive from a ready-meals company that made a £50m profit in the last year admitted with some sadness that 27 per cent of their sales were now single-portion meals. He was disappointed because the company's founding mission had been to make interesting, pleasant, high-quality meals for busy people who wanted to entertain friends and family. The name of that executive? Wordsworth.

Twenty-Two

Paradise Lost
(1667)
John Milton (1608–1674)

John Milton had an angelic face. You can see it still in London's National Gallery. At Cambridge he had a nickname to match, the Lady of Christ's College. Not especially snappy, but it does the job. Yet he spent more time than any other English poet thinking about hell.

He lost a close childhood friend, Charles Diodati, who was only about thirty when he died. He was separated from his first wife, seventeen-year-old Mary Powell, within weeks of their marriage, wrote a famous defence of divorce, and although they were reconciled and had three daughters, she later died in childbirth, their only son dying too at about fifteen months. His second wife, Katherine Woodcock, also died within months of giving birth to their daughter, also named Katherine, who died shortly after her mother. His marriage to Katherine lasted about two years. Milton had to bring up his surviving three daughters, largely by himself, and aged around forty-four, he went totally blind. He survived plague and civil war, was briefly imprisoned, but was somehow spared the barbaric, grisly fate of other regicides. Remarkable when you consider he was virtually the official mouthpiece for those who put Charles I to death. 'If you're going through hell, keep going' are words attributed to Winston Churchill during Second World War. Milton would have appreciated the sentiment.

Paradise Lost is an experience. It belittles it to call it a poem, even an epic poem. It starts literally with a journey into hell and ends with Adam and Eve walking sorrowfully out of the Garden of Eden, holding hands like small children. It's an investigation into what it means to be human. In between we witness violence and war on such a scale that even Hollywood hasn't yet managed to sell it, although there have been rumours for years. When Michael and Satan fight, angel to angel in Book VI, they make *Transformers* look like kittens squabbling over a ball of wool. It will take more than an army of CGI artists to do justice to the monumentally Baroque nature of Milton's imagination.

It would be a confident actor indeed who thinks he can play the role of Milton's Satan. If, like me, you find all those articles about how much of a strain playing Hamlet has been on the latest star to take on the role – how they only managed with some intense psychotherapy and Reiki massage sessions in a yurt in Nepal – a bit tedious, then you will appreciate exactly what I mean when I say Milton's Satan isn't much of a starring role, more a black hole. Yet I've no doubt that, as I write, there are probably bona fide film stars cooing about how much they love the latest script circulating in Los Angeles but whose grasp of Milton's character is about as firm as Wile E. Coyote's hold on

Road Runner's neck. It will take more than a read-through of the *Acme Book of Acting* to prepare anyone to shape one syllable of the toxic words Milton puts into Satan's foul mouth so effectively.

Paradise Lost is full of artistic achievements most sensible artists would baulk at. Milton not only describes hell for us, he explains what it feels like to be there. In the same way he is not the least frightened of depicting Adam and Eve's physical perfection nor the blissful garden God creates for them. He is as bold about emotions as he is about place. He doesn't shy away from handling the sex. He takes us inside Satan's head and no one who reads the poem should ever underestimate him when he says in the opening passage, he intends to *justify the ways of God to men*.

Paradise Lost is not merely an exercise in theodicy, in explaining how an essentially loving God can permit evil, it's a measure of how unshakeable Milton's faith was. It is what he believed to be true. Staggering achievements when you remember he was also blind. We still don't know how he avoided the humiliation of stumbling, blind, up the steps to the scaffold. Milton could so easily have been a Protestant martyr.

Once considered arguably the central poem in the entire English literary canon, *Paradise Lost* has become so alien to modern students and readers it is rarely studied in schools and often in universities at nothing more than a cursory level. This is, of course, partly a side effect of the dramatic shift from a predominantly passive Christian culture to an almost aggressively secular one I have witnessed in my own lifetime. The orgy of materialism and self-gratifying hedonism today that characterises the central spiritual event of the Christian calendar, Christmas, is all you need to tell you that. If you know nothing or little of the Bible and classical literature, then there are numerous references to names and events in *Paradise Lost* that will be a foreign language. But it's easy to overestimate this relatively low hurdle. Milton was no ordinary scholar and few of his contemporaries would have read the poem without having to do more than a little rooting around in their personal libraries. In Book VII he makes this point crystal clear himself, when seeking help from his muse Urania . . . *still govern though my song,/Urania, and fit audience find, though few.* He knew this book was never going to appear in the window at Waterstones, surrounded by posters of Raphael and spirit glasses with *Gin & Miltonic* written on them.

Characters like Uzziel and Ithuriel, two angels who catch Satan in the act of whispering to Eve in her sleep, are not biblical but belong to a rabbinical tradition only a Hebrew scholar like Milton would have known about. The poem is full of names of people and places readers will not recognise but which really shouldn't deter anyone. Milton was essentially a scholar, as his reading demonstrates. University libraries are full of books detailing the influence of Homer, Lucan, Lucretius, Ovid and Virgil on *Paradise Lost*, but Milton's reading embraced a much wider circle of classical authors, including Apollonius of Rhodes, Aratus, Dionysius Periegetes, Hesiod, Nicander, Quintus Smyrnaeus and Oppian. Apart from the fact that most modern editions will be well glossed, much of the mythology and exotic nomenclature he pillages from these writers is there precisely because it is exotic, because Milton needs it to take his readers' minds away from bustling, dirty, familiar London streets and out from under their thatched roofs if he is to get them to think about heaven and hell.

As with all poetry, your willingness to engage with it matters. As already discussed when thinking about how best to read *The Prelude*, my advice for anyone who thinks *Paradise Lost* might be too difficult is to be pragmatic and rely on the dozens of skilful editors and academics who have devoted many hours to honing the punctuation of any edition you are likely to read today. Stick firmly and determinedly to the sentence as the single unit that will see you through, and push on through it, even when you may feel unsure. Stick slavishly to the punctuation and read slightly faster than you might normally read anything. It's fatal to lean the opposite way and think, more logically, that slow and steady wins the race. I found an online version of the complete poem performed live by a sequence of leading academics and poets that did just this and that was so painful to listen to I abandoned it after the first book. It is an indictment of how poorly poetry has been served educationally in recent decades that such a weak performance is somehow deemed acceptable enough to share. There are moments when you can actually hear the reader failing to understand, like a primary schoolchild with a finger shifting clumsily across the page under unfamiliar syllables. All I can imagine in their defence was that the various readers didn't rehearse at all. In itself that says something about the poetry community.

Believe in yourself and don't fall for the lie that *Paradise Lost* is only for the chosen few. If you need to stop when you get to the end of a sentence, then stop. Like Wordsworth, Milton is quite capable of crafting sentences that run on for many lines and because he was a brilliant Latinist, his sentence structure often reflects that, and can sound awkward to English ears. Verbs especially appear in all sorts of unexpected places. Even other poets have complained, most famously T. S. Eliot, no slouch himself when it came to classical literature. But if you place your trust in the editors you will find very little of the poem that troubling and, more importantly, you can enjoy all its greatest passages and achievements.

   And there is no shortage. In the very first book Satan gathers together a vast host of fallen angels in hell to debate how best to continue their war with heaven before they disperse like colossal ants across a landscape so cruelly inhospitable I defy anyone not to sympathise, yet from its punishing, base materials they construct an immense unholy palace, the infamous Pandemonium. In Book II Satan journeys to hell's gates to confront Death, the offspring of his incestuous rape of Sin, his own daughter. Both Sin and Death are borderline insane creations, the stuff of incurable nightmare, daubed on the wall of an asylum. Sin is a woman, beautiful down to the waist, where her shape *ended foul in many a scaly fold,/Voluminous and vast.* Inside her womb *A cry of hell hounds* hide and bark, bursting out to threaten and attack, themselves the progeny of her rape by Death, her own son. Death is a shapeless horror, a paradoxical combination of substance and shadow, *Fierce as ten Furies, terrible as hell*, a crown his only identifying feature, and eternally insatiable greed and hunger his constant yearnings. It is a measure of Milton's genius that he portrays Death not as violent or overwhelming, but as almost pitiable, tormented by a hunger so unimaginably vast that he can never be satisfied.

Horror in film and literature has become commonplace today. Just another form of entertainment separated from *Strictly Come Dancing* and *The Great British Bake Off* by nothing more substantial than a few minutes on a TV schedule. It's a genre I have never understood and have avoided all my life, yet somehow it insinuates its way into otherwise creditable drama and all kinds of visual media as seamlessly as a soundtrack. But even the most enthusiastic fans of the grisly and macabre are likely to swallow uncomfortably once Milton's Sin and Death take hold of their imagination and mingle inextricably with their real lives. He doesn't offer them for our entertainment. He gives them a history and home, a place in the universe we all inhabit that is as tangible as it is terrible. To read *Paradise Lost* is to find Sin and Death make sense of trench warfare, the Twin Towers and every mass shooting journalists and politicians routinely wring their limp hands over. Plague and a brutal civil war left little room for horror as entertainment in Milton's England.

Paradise Lost is not something you snuggle up in the corner of your favourite armchair to read like a good detective novel, wrapped in a blankie and armed with a mug of cocoa. This is not a comfortable, comforting read. Milton was writing because by writing, by enduring all the messy mental trial and error required before his various amanuenses could even put a single word down on paper, he was reaching an understanding. Think of the hours and hours of media interviews, the panel discussions and news items on nominally important issues that flood out on a rapidly burgeoning range of channels we can access instantly via our phones, or on any number of other devices, and compare the combined effort that goes into the production of news to the efforts Milton made to understand. It is literally chaos in comparison, the very term Milton uses to describe the vast emptiness between hell and earth Satan has to battle through in order to tempt Eve and give mankind over to Sin and Death. It's a reminder of just how deeply poets think.

It's far less fashionable today to think hard about difficult matters. The noun for it, *mentation*, is almost unheard of. It's so common to do the opposite today and reach for the single most unimpeachable word from the politically correct lexicon to stifle all debate, that even humanity's most intellectual institutions, universities, have succumbed to pressures to shy away from uncomfortable thinking in favour of safe spaces. I am acutely aware Milton's intricate verse may feel like a genuinely alien, distinctly daunting challenge. Even a good education may not have equipped a reader for the imaginative demands Milton's own imagination makes of them. Knowing what to expect from a writer is often a sensible and rational reason for taking them off the bookshelf. Milton doesn't offer you that security. Instead he urges you to think as deeply as he does himself, but I can assure you, that invitation is worth sticking behind the clock on anyone's mantelpiece.

Milton held a key diplomatic post in the parliamentary

government that Oliver Cromwell briefly led after the execution of Charles I. He was appointed Secretary for Foreign Tongues in 1649, partly because he was a brilliant Latin scholar and all foreign correspondence at this time was carried out in Latin. But before working for Cromwell's government he had already earned a reputation as a republican polemicist through a number of works, including one called *Areopagitica*, which is still used by people today to argue against censorship and for freedom of expression. Ironically, it was Cromwell's government that introduced the strictest censorship England has ever seen. But Milton, writing in *Areopagitica*, had this to say about literature and why it matters.

> ... *as good almost kill a Man as kill a good Book; who kills a Man kills a reasonable creature, Gods Image; but hee who destroyes a good Booke, kills reason it selfe, kills the Image of God, as it were in the eye. Many a man lives a burden to the Earth; but a good Booke is the pretious life-blood of a master spirit, imbalm'd and treasur'd up on purpose to a life beyond life.*[1]

I hope all I need to add is that *Paradise Lost* is a very good book indeed. Just how good is easily illustrated by this extract taken from Book I, in which Milton introduces us, and Satan, to hell.

> Nine times the space that measures day and night   50
> To mortal men, he, with his horrid crew,
> Lay vanquished, rolling in the fiery gulf,

Confounded, though immortal: but his doom
Reserved him to more wrath; for now the thought
Both of lost happiness and lasting pain   55
Torments him; round he throws his baleful eyes,
That witnessed huge affliction and dismay,
Mixed with obdurate pride and steadfast hate;
At once, as far as angel's ken, he views
The dismal situation waste and wild: 60
A dungeon horrible, on all sides round,
As one great furnace flamed, yet from those flames
No light, but rather darkness visible
Served only to discover sights of woe,
Regions of sorrow, doleful shades, where peace   65
And rest can never dwell, hope never comes
That comes to all, but torture without end
Still urges, and a fiery deluge, fed
With ever-burning sulphur unconsumed:
Such place eternal justice had prepared   70
For those rebellious; here their prison ordained
In utter darkness, and their portion set,
As far removed from God and light of heaven
As from the centre thrice to the utmost pole.[2]

From the start Milton strikes a clever balance between hell as physical and spiritual torment. The unique status Satan and the fallen angels have as immortal but impotent is immediately clear. Satan's pain is always as much psychological as it is physical, so *lost happiness* and *lasting pain* are inseparable. Satan is never allowed by Milton to forget he has been cast out of heaven. Hell is as much the absence of God's love as it is a peculiarly geographical domain created specially by him to contain the damned. Knowledge of his condition, no matter how he reasons himself into continued opposition to God's will and how many of the fallen he convinces, lies at the heart of Satan's punishment. The scale of his loss is immense and part of Milton's achievement is how well he conveys that idea here and throughout the entire poem, especially when Satan reaches earth and first sets eyes on Adam and Eve. The mere sight of man causes him intense sorrow and agony.

> *Oh hell! What do mine eyes with grief behold?*
> *Into our room of bliss this high advanced*
> *Creatures of other mould – earth-born perhaps,*
> *Not spirits, yet to heavenly spirits bright*
> *Little inferior – whom my thoughts could pursue*
> *With wonder, and could love; so lively shines*
> *In then divine resemblance, and such grace*
> *The hand that formed them on their shape hath poured.*[3]

Yet Satan quickly suppresses these emotions, exchanging them for his eternal enmity of God, allowing him to treat Adam and Eve not just as collateral damage, but as a target he can delight in destroying. By the end of Book IX he has successfully persuaded Eve to eat the forbidden fruit and destroyed Paradise for ever, turning it into a playground for Sin and Death. How he does that is what has always most intrigued me about *Paradise*

Lost, because it's so beautifully simple. He lies. One carefully worded, elaborate lie is all Satan uses to condemn mankind to suffering. The serpent tells Eve it was by eating the fruit that he gained the power of speech, and the wisdom and knowledge that comes with it, raising him alone amongst the animals to the same level as man. This is untrue, yet crucially it is because she *believes* the serpent that Eve reasons herself into a position where she has no fear of the forbidden fruit and subsequently eats it.

Milton's clarity about this invites us to reflect on the part duplicity plays in modern culture and society. Our businesses and industries thrive on manipulating images and language to drive sales and generate profit. It's normal, acceptable practice. Our politicians regard the act of lying as a political strategy and adopt euphemisms to disguise it, like spin. We apotheosise the leading exponents of the one profession that thrives on lying, acting, devoting the pages of glossy magazines and hours of television to international events described as ceremonies, in which they are richly rewarded for their ability to deceive, at the same time laughing incredulously at the way they heap praise on each other.

Both the USA and the UK recently broke out in a cold sweat over a suspicion that two major democratic events – the election of Donald Trump and the British vote to leave the EU – may have been influenced by lies and deceit perpetrated by a foreign government and disseminated widely online as part of a new Cold War. The very notion that we are all the victims of lying we can't identify or locate is what lies behind the concept of fake news.

If ever there was a poem fit for an age, *Paradise Lost* is made for the twenty-first century.

Our modern faith in technology is, ironically, almost alchemical in its scale and ambition. There is almost nothing we don't believe it can accomplish, no magic trick we don't think it can pull off. The keenest advocates of this new kind of alchemical thinking would probably love Book XI of *Paradise Lost*. The archangel Michael literally shows Adam the future. It's a future that begins with the horror of fratricide, Cain's murder of his brother Abel, includes visions of numerous ways to die and the terrible diseases Adam and Eve's disobedience has loosed on mankind, peaceful luxury and excess, as well as full-scale war, and ends with Noah, the flood and God's covenant with man, the rainbow. But don't be fooled by *those coloured streaks in heaven*. Eve is literally put to sleep by Michael, unfit for all that manly horizon-scanning, *Let Eve (for I have drenched her eyes)/Here sleep below while thou to foresight wak'st*.

Yet in spite of the way Eve is treated by Michael in Book XI, the relationship between Adam and Eve, the intricate, subtle conversations they have before and after sinning, are ironically some of the most fruitful sections of the poem to dwell on. If you're the kind of reader who enjoys writers who think hard about how men and women treat each other, you will find lots to reflect on in what Adam and Eve say to each other. He doesn't dote and she is no fool.

It would be a real mistake to take Michael's hypnotic trick as indicative of the poem's treatment of femininity as a whole. Milton is far too clever for that, as no doubt his three wives would concur, had they the chance, although biographers have been intensely frustrated by a lack of credible written material to helps us understand his relationships with his three daughters or his three wives. Rumour abounds, as is its natural tendency, but real evidence of how happy or unhappy they all were will be found on a dusty, stately home bookshelf somewhere, next to a copy of an unknown play by Shakespeare.

Milton is so unlike Shakespeare in this. Both poets left almost nothing tangible behind them for historians and critics to weave into anything like a substantial biography. Yet while Shakespeare's personality is invisible, Milton's is stamped all over his work like inky thumbprints. Perhaps we shouldn't be surprised, since he was such an overtly political writer. When you read *Paradise Lost* there is always this radical, ferociously intelligent, Protestant republican lurking somewhere in the shadows over your shoulder. It's a bit uncomfortable, like being in an exam room stalked by watchful teachers and even though you would never dream of cheating, worrying in case they suspect you are.

There are a number of reasons why I saved *Paradise Lost* for last, primarily, of course, because this book was designed to break down readers' aversion to verse in manageable steps. We've come a long way together from Sonnet 18 and 'The Hawk'. But one key reason has to do with something that has taken up most of my life, education. Milton's parents valued it and made sure their son received the best they could afford. Mine did too. We were both lucky. Today developed nations spend billions of dollars on it at home and abroad, yet millions of children worldwide receive no education at all, and millions more who do still struggle to understand what they read.

In a November 2017 article for the *New York Times*, Dan Willingham, a psychology professor at the University of Virginia, complained powerfully about poor levels of literacy in the USA. He argued that things are not much better today than when the USA last ran a national assessment of adult literacy in 2003. Then, *in comparing two newspaper editorials with different interpretations of scientific evidence or examining a table to evaluate credit card offers—95 per cent failed.*[4] After thinking about the various ways literacy is taught in the USA, he makes the point that *comprehension is intimately intertwined with knowledge* before finally concluding that concerned readers of the *New York Times*, who no doubt consider themselves highly literate, should not *blame the internet, or smartphones, or fake news for Americans' poor reading. Blame ignorance.*[5]

Yet anyone who reads extensively about modern culture can't fail but detect a widely held confidence that those of us living and writing today are clearly better educated, and therefore wiser, than previous generations. Our remarkable scientific and technological achievements appear to clearly demonstrate this and, in themselves, echo back the belief that we are so much cleverer than everyone else. It's a lie Milton's Satan would have been immensely proud to call his own.

My limited scientific reading from the past has included books like Robert Burton's seventeenth-century *Anatomy of Melancholy*, so I'm happy to concede centuries of scientific and psychological study have indeed proven ideas about bile and phlegm, and numerous other scientific red herrings, to be flawed. But my reading has also included lots of poetry. There is nothing ignorant in Homer or Virgil, nothing dull-witted about Sappho or Donne. I suspect as individual representatives of Homo sapiens, we are no wiser than when we first started to decorate the walls of caves and tell stories round camp fires. *Paradise Lost*, because its religious and theological preoccupations are so extreme, its universe so strange and difficult, is the perfect antidote to modern intellectual narcissism. I defy anyone who reads *Paradise Lost* to think Milton a fool.

Between chapters on *The Prelude* and *Paradise Lost* my mother died. She beat me at Scrabble the day before her 99-year-old body climbed out of bed and fainted. Within five days, her physical form was like a much-loved paperback novel, so loosely bound that a breeze finding its way into the room where she was fighting to stay alive would have scattered it irreparably. She hated draughts. Her 100-year-old brother was taken into hospital the same day and died a little over twenty-four hours before her. Death and birth, like falling in and out of love, seem to crave poetry. Since then I have read and re-read John Donne's 'Holy Sonnet VI', 'This is my play's last scene'. Why? because it makes me feel better. Here it is simply because one day it may comfort you too.

> *This is my play's last scene; here heavens appoint*
> *My pilgrimage's last mile; and my race,*
> *Idly, yet quickly run, hath this last pace,*
> *My span's last inch, my minute's latest point;*

And gluttonous death will instantly unjoint
My body and my soul, and I shall sleep a space;
But my ever-waking part shall see that face
Whose fear already shakes my every joint.
Then, as my soul to heaven, her first seat, takes flight,
And earth-born body in the earth shall dwell,
So fall my sins, that all may have their right,
To where they are bred, and would press me, to hell.
Impute me righteous, thus purg'd of evil,
For thus I leave the world, the flesh, the devil.

Where to Now?

My original thought at this point was to offer you some conclusions, the conventional way any author ends a book, when they aren't intent on selling you a sequel. But then I realised that if I've succeeded in what I set out to do, if those astoundingly creative, imaginative word artists I'd introduced you to have communicated with you in the ways they and I had hoped when we both started arranging words in carefully constructed lines of verse and prose, then you would be sitting here now thinking, quite rightly, 'What now?'

It's a rare, but joyful pleasure to reach the end of a book and feel disappointment. A friend once told me how, as she turned the final page of Anthony Powell's *Hearing Secret Harmonies*, the last in his beautiful series of twelve novels, *A Dance to the Music of Time*, she became tearful because she realised she would never have that pleasure in quite the same way ever again. The many hours of her life she had surrendered to the spell cast by Powell's prose, haunting his characters inside those book covers, invisibly and silently watching whole chunks of their lives being lived, was gone for ever.

I really hope you feel disappointed. Nothing would please me more than to know you have reached this point only to feel a little lost, as though you don't quite know where to turn next because one poet after another has taken you on a journey you simply don't want to end; mapless rather than hapless.

The easiest direction to take, and in some ways the obvious one, is to retrace your steps to those poets whose poems most intrigued or engaged you, and seek out more of their work to enjoy. Isaac Rosenberg didn't live long enough to write much, so his entire collected works would only keep you busy for an hour or so. Though a more prolific writer, Edward Thomas's life was also cut short by the Great War, while the far more hardy Thomas published around a thousand poems before he died, aged eighty-seven. Reading his collected poems would entertain you for weeks. Opt for Coleridge or Keats and I defy you not to end up reading more than the poetry they wrote, while it's entirely possible to devote one's life to reading Shakespeare or Milton; many literary scholars have.

Another tactic you might try is to read more of the type of poetry you most enjoy. That can lead you to all kinds of unexpected places because love poetry, for example, doesn't just occupy a period in history in which courtiers regarded it as something you really had to have on your CV. In marked contrast, war poetry is almost wholly constrained historically by that small band of young men whose lives were defined by that one Great War that slaughtered them and their companions in their thousands, often in a matter of minutes. Homer's a bit of an exception, but if you use the phrase 'war poetry' to guide your search it will inevitably lead you to a far narrower group of poets than a search for 'love poems' or 'nature poetry' might do.

You might even choose to stray off the map completely and read poetry in translation. The English aren't the only race to produce great poets, but a word of caution; as any professional translator will tell you, it's impossible to translate a poem well from one language to another. Imagine the headache facing a French translator of this verse by Gerard Manley Hopkins, which I quoted in chapter ten.

> *Left hand, off land, I hear the lark ascend,*
> *His rash-fresh re-winded new-skeinèd score*
> *In crisps of curl off wild winch whirl, and pour*
> *And pelt music, till none's to spill nor spend.*

The best anyone can do is rewrite it. It takes a rare and special kind of skill to do even that well, but that doesn't mean that poets like Rainer Maria Rilke, Stéphane Mallarmé, Alexander Pushkin or even Dante Alighieri are out of bounds. It just means you will never quite be able to enjoy what a native German, French, Russian or Italian speaker is likely to enjoy from their works. What on earth would a non-English speaker make of the remarkable, carefully rhymed, quintessentially English verse of a poet like John Betjeman. Take a look at the opening of his a poem 'Crematorium' if you need further convincing.

Just in case, after all my efforts to encourage your delight in reading works by Seamus Heaney, Christina Rossetti, Rita Dove, Coleridge and all the others, doubt may still be tinkling faintly somewhere in the back of your mind, like a wind chime at the far end of the garden, then finally, reflect on this. With the exception of touch, mathematics and possibly music, which is really maths practised by artists, the only way we have of communicating anything is through words. Our individual lives are imprisoned and enriched by the language that we use, the words we exchange with others. Poetry is where the possibilities happen. It is the way humans test what language can do, not just to breaking point, but beyond. Without it we are vulnerable to those who weaponise and wield words for political or personal purposes. It is our only bulwark against barbarity.

Which is why it is endlessly fascinating, continually surprising and, more than anything else, capable of distilling beauty. I smile more because I read poetry, I am moved to tears more too and possibly argue more intensely than most people would about middling, as well as momentous things. In the great and even not so great outdoors, I notice more. Two magpies flying out of a claret-and-gold autumnal horse chestnut tree win my attention. A skein of Canada geese passing only fifteen metres or so above my head in a suburban street raise my eyes and thoughts heavenwards. The squelch of sodden moss under my boots on the edge of a wild Scottish river, the livid, marker-pen pinks and lime greens of all that vegetation under my feet, entrances me almost as much as the tiny, wet-furred, bustling vole that scuttles inches from my boot. This morning, walking my dog routinely in a suburban street, I stood under a silver birch tree while tiny seeds dropped all around me like the first feathery snowflakes of a winter fall. All these things I have seen and felt just in the past few weeks.

Poetry has been, and is, a way for me to understand my life better and because of that, I believe those closest to me benefit too. However gripped and deeply engrossed I am in a fiction by Dickens or Turgenev, the novel doesn't do this for me, neither does the mystery or hysteria of the theatre. Poetry is a unique creative gift from one human being to many others. It's the white sheet of thought. And the point of poetry is to proffer that white sheet.

Credits

'The Hawk' by George Mackay Brown. Copyright © 2005 Estate of George Mackay Brown. Reproduced by permission of John Murray Press, a division of Hodder and Stoughton Limited.

'The General' by Seigfried Sassoon. Copyright Siegfried Sassoon reproduced by kind permission of the Estate of George Sassoon.

'Mrs Midas' by Carol Ann Duffy. 'Mrs Midas' from *The World's Wife* by Carol Ann Duffy. Published by Picador, 1999. Copyright © Carol Ann Duffy. Reproduced by permission of the author c/o Rogers Coleridge & White Ltd., 20 Powis Mews, London W11 1JN

'Famous for What?' by Holly McNish. This poem was commissioned by The Economist Educational Foundation, the independent charity from the *Economist* newspaper. The Foundation runs the Burnet News Club, a programme for state schools which develops students' critical thinking and literacy skills through discussions about the news. Reproduced with permission.

'The Gun' by Vicki Feaver. From *The Book of Blood* by Vicki Feaver. Published by Jonathan Cape. Reprinted by permission of The Random House Group Limited. © 2006.

'Blackberry-Picking' by Seamus Heaney, from *Death of a Naturalist*, reproduced with kind permission of Faber and Faber Ltd.

'The Bistro Styx' by Rita Dove. Copyright © 1995 by Rita Dove, from COLLECTED POEMS: 1974–2004 by Rita Dove. Used by permission of W. W. Norton & Company, Inc.

Sources

'Twickenham Garden' by John Donne, *Donne: A Selection of His Poetry*, edited by John Hayward, Penguin, 1988, p.41.

'The Sea and the Skylark' Gerard Manley Hopkins, *Poems and Prose*, edited by W. H. Gardner, Penguin 1975, p.29.

The Prelude by William Wordsworth, University of Cambridge online collections, https://sms.cam.ac.uk/collection/1170406.

Paradise Lost by John Milton, *Paradise Lost*, edited by Alastair Fowler, Second Edition, Pearson, 2007.

'Holy Sonnet VI' by John Donne, *Donne: A Selection of His Poetry*, edited by John Hayward, Penguin, 1988, p.168.

All poems not listed above were sourced from the Poetry Foundation, poetryfoundation.org.

Notes

Chapter 7

1 www.poetryfoundation.org/poems-and-poets/poets/detail/christina-rossetti

Chapter 9

1 Thomas Hardy, *The Trumpet Major*, London, Macmillan, 1974, p. 158.
2 www.theguardian.com/books/2017/apr/11/unseen-sylvia-plath-letters-claim-domestic-abuse-by-ted-hughes?CMP=fb_gu accessed 5 June 2017.

Chapter 10

1 Benvenuto Cellini, *The Autobiography of Benvenuto Cellini*, London, Penguin Books Ltd, revised edition, 1998, p. 245.
2 A reproduction of the original book available from the Internet Archive, archive.org/details/cu31924013443050 accessed 13 June 2017.

Chapter 11

1. Derek Hirst & Stephen N. Zwicker, *Andrew Marvell: Orphan of the Hurricane*, London, OUP, 2012, p. 133.

Chapter 12

1. www.bbc.co.uk/programmes/b08tv8fb, accessed 18 June 2017.
2. www.huffingtonpost.co.uk/james-mahon/british-poet-hollie-mcnish_b_3432059.html, accessed 18 June 2017.
3. www.economistfoundation.org/wp-content/uploads/2015/01/Poems-by-Hollie-McNish-Famous-for-what.pdf, accessed 18 June 2017.
4. *PN Review*, Volume 44, Number 3, January–February 2018.
5. https://www.youtube.com/watch?v=JcoVqwKuJHY
6. www.huffingtonpost.co.uk/james-mahon/british-poet-hollie-mcnish_b_3432059.html, accessed 18 June 2017.

Chapter 13

1. www.poetryarchive.org/poem/gun accessed 26 June 2017.
2. Adrienne Rich, *Blood, Bread and Poetry: The Location of the Poet, The Massachusetts Review*, Vol. 24, No. 3 (Autumn, 1983), p. 253.

Chapter 14

1. A. L. Clements (ed.), *Johns Donne's Poetry*, New York, W. W. Norton and Company 1966, p. 110.

Chapter 16

1 web.cs.ucdavis.edu/~rogaway/classes/188/materials/postman.pdf accessed 18 July 2017.

Chapter 18

1 Jack Stillenger, *Reading The Eve of St Agnes: The Multiples of Complex Literary Transaction*, New York, Oxford, OUP, 1999, p. 22.
2 Ibid., p. 22.

Chapter 20

1 W. H. Gardner, *Gerard Manley Hopkins Poems and Prose*, London, Penguin, 1953, p. xv.
2 Ibid., p. xxii.
3 Ibid., p. 195.

Chapter 21

1 Wordsworth rewrote *The Prelude* and there are several versions. Academics tend to agree the 1805 version is the best.
2 www.tes.com/news/school-news/breaking-views/learning-how-write-poetry-seriously-not-a-subject-suitable-a-school, accessed 21 September 2017.
3 sms.cam.ac.uk/collection/1170406. I have used this online version produced by Cambridge University for all quotations. Book I, ll. 1–67.
4 sms.cam.ac.uk/collection/1170406. I have used this resource for all quotations. Book II, ll.310–33.
5 sms.cam.ac.uk/collection/1170406, Book VIII, ll. 848–65.

6 sms.cam.ac.uk/collection/1170406, Book VII, ll. 234–44.
7 sms.cam.ac.uk/collection/1170406, Book XIII, line 410.
8 sms.cam.ac.uk/collection/1170406, Book IX, ll. 64–80.
9 sms.cam.ac.uk/collection/1170406, Book X, ll. 46–54.
10 sms.cam.ac.uk/collection/1170406, Book II , ll. 216–26.
11 Richard Dawkins, *The Blind Watchmaker*, London, Penguin, 1991 p. 111.
12 https://sms.cam.ac.uk/collection/1170406, Book XIII, ll. 717–47.
13 sms.cam.ac.uk/collection/1170406, Book XIII, ll. 446–54.
14 sms.cam.ac.uk/collection/1170406, Book XII, ll. 194–204.

Chapter 22

1 www.dartmouth.edu/~milton/reading_room/areopagitica/text.html, accessed 6 November 2017.
2 John Milton, *Complete English Poems, Of Education, Areopagitica,* editor, Gordon Campbell, London, Everyman, 1990, Book I, p. 151.
3 Ibid. Book IV, p. 232.
4 Daniel T. Willingham, 'How to Get Your Mind to Read', *New York Times*, 25 November 2017.
5 Ibid.

Acknowledgements

I'd like to thank Unbound but most especially Georgia Odd for her experienced advice about funding and Philip Connor for having faith in the original idea, and for bringing such a sensible, balanced eye to bear on my first draft. I'd also like to thank Kate Quarry and Imogen Denny for all their patience and hard work, editing what turned out to be quite a complicated manuscript.

A Note on the Author

Joe Nutt is a former teacher with almost twenty years of English teaching experience. He has written books on Shakespeare, John Donne and most recently a guidebook to *Paradise Lost*. He is now one of the leading educationalists in the UK and writes a fortnightly column for the *Times Educational Supplement*.

Unbound
Liberating ideas

Unbound is the world's first crowdfunding publisher, established in 2011.

We believe that wonderful things can happen when you clear a path for people who share a passion. That's why we've built a platform that brings together readers and authors to crowdfund books they believe in – and give fresh ideas that don't fit the traditional mould the chance they deserve.

This book is in your hands because readers made it possible. Everyone who pledged their support is listed below. Join them by visiting unbound.com and supporting a book today.

Maggie Attfield	Paul Kavanagh	Madeleine Nutt
Lisa Bolgar Smith	Dan Kieran	Will Orr-Ewing
Tom Burkard	Stuart Lee	Dan Peters
Lyndsey Caldwell	Colin McKenzie	Mark Phillips
Daisy Christodoulou	Ken McKinnon	Justin Pollard
John Clark	John Mitchinson	Mark Ramsden
Claire Coupe	Zuzana Miyahara Kratka	Maggie Reed
Jonathan Davies		Kurt Roosen
Diane Foster	Carlo Navato	Clare Shepherd
Elaine Halligan	Josh Nieboer	John Towers
Angus Harper	Anthony Nutt	John Waldron
Katie Ivens	Eleanor Nutt	Amy White

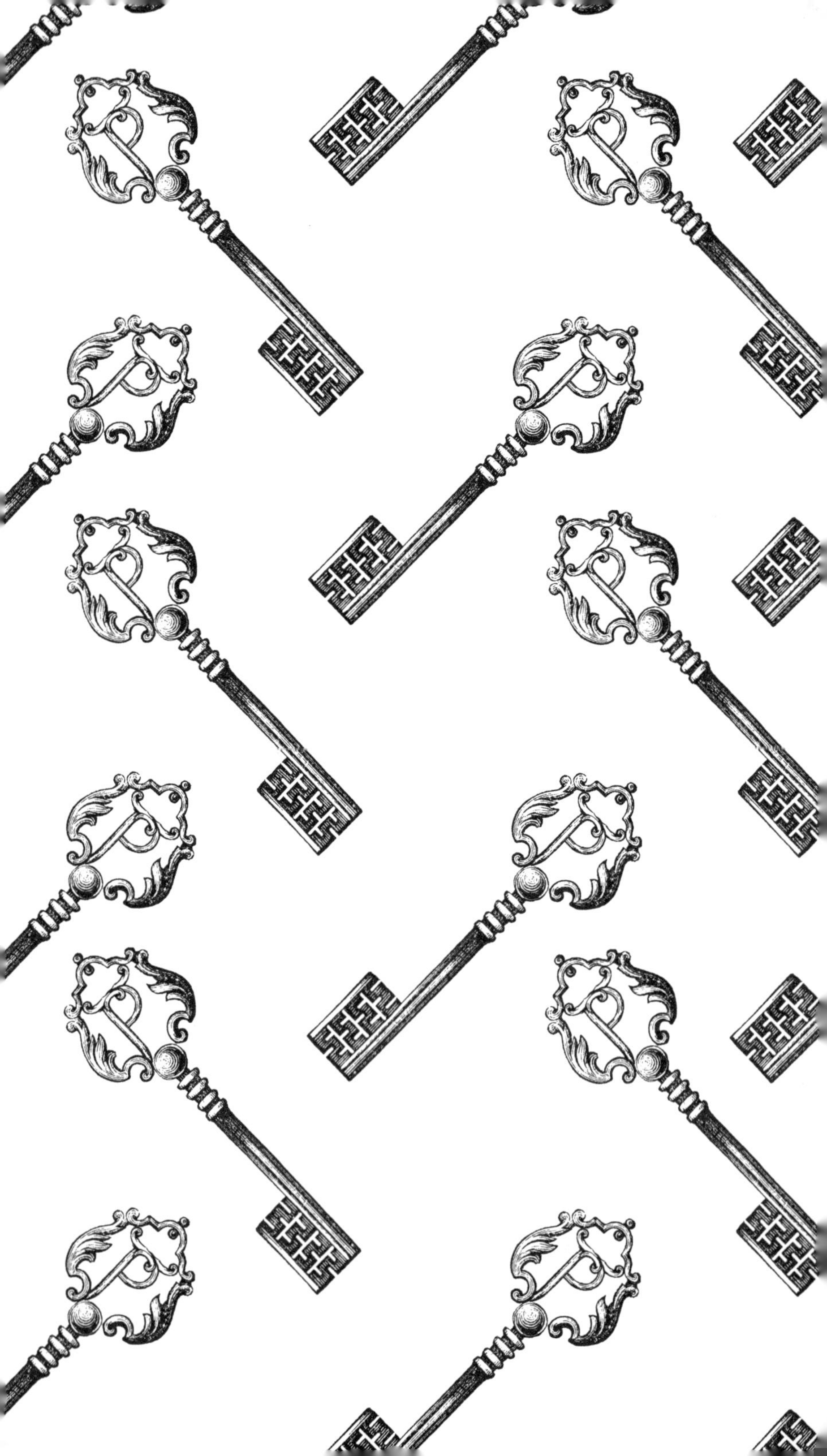